MANIPULATING LIFE

Debating The Genetic Revolution

Gary E. McCuen

IDEAS IN CONFLICT SERIES

publications inc.

411 Mallalieu Drive
Hudson, Wisconsin 54016

Illustration & photo credits
Department of the Army 121, Daily World 108, Scott Long, *The Minneapolis Star & Tribune* 34, Office of Technology Assessment 66, 70, 76, 80, 84, 93, 103, 114, Mike Peters, *Dayton Daily News* 97, President's Commission for the Study of Ethical Problems in Medicine and Biomedical and Behavioral Research 13, 25, 31, 38, 50, *Imprimis* 19—This drawing was reprinted by permission from *Imprimis,* the monthly journal of Hillsdale College, featuring presentations at Hillsdale's Center for Constructive Alternatives and at its Shavano Institute for National Leadership.

©1985 by Gary E. McCuen Publications, Inc.
411 Mallalieu Drive ● Hudson, Wisconsin 54016 ●
(715) 386-5662
International Standard Book Number 0-86596-054-2
Printed in the United States of America

CONTENTS

REASONING SKILL DEVELOPMENT

These activities may be used as individualized study guides for students in libraries and resource centers or as discussion catalysts in small group and classroom discussions.

IDEAS in CONFLICT ®

This series features ideas in conflict on political, social and moral issues. It presents counterpoints, debates, opinions, commentary and analysis for use in libraries and classrooms. Each title in the series uses one or more of the following basic elements:

Introductions that present an issue overview giving historic background and/or a description of the controversy.

Counterpoints and debates carefully chosen from publications, books, and position papers on the political right and left to help librarians and teachers respond to requests that treatment of public issues be fair and balanced.

Symposiums and forums that go beyond debates that can polarize and oversimplify. These present commentary from across the political spectrum that reflect how complex issues attract many shades of opinion.

A global emphasis with foreign perspectives and surveys on various moral questions and political issues that will help readers to place subject matter in a less culture-bound and ethno-centric frame of reference. In an ever shrinking and interdependent world, understanding and cooperation are essential. Many issues are global in nature and can be effectively dealt with only by common efforts and international understanding.

Reasoning skill study guides and discussion activities provide ready made tools for helping with critical reading and evaluation of content. The guides and activities deal with one or more of the following:

RECOGNIZING AUTHOR'S POINT OF VIEW

INTERPRETING EDITORIAL CARTOONS

VALUES IN CONFLICT

WHAT IS EDITORIAL BIAS?

6

WHAT IS SEX BIAS?

WHAT IS POLITICAL BIAS?

WHAT IS ETHNOCENTRIC BIAS?

WHAT IS RACE BIAS?

WHAT IS RELIGIOUS BIAS?

From across *the political spectrum* varied sources are presented for research projects and classroom discussions. Diverse opinions in the series come from magazines, newspapers, syndicated columnists, books, political speeches, foreign nations, and position papers by corporations and non-profit institutions.

About the Editor

Gary E. McCuen is an editor and publisher of anthologies for public libraries and curriculum materials for schools. Over the past 14 years his publications of over 200 titles have specialized in social, moral and political conflict. They include books, pamphlets, cassettes, tabloids, filmstrips and simulation games, many of them designed from his curriculums during 11 years of teaching junior and senior high school social studies. At present he is the editor and publisher of the *Ideas in Conflict* series and the *Editorial Forum* series.

GENETIC ENGINEERING

Albert Gore, Jr.

In the mid-19th century, a scientist and monk named Gregor Mendel conducted a series of experiments on ordinary garden peas. In his experiments Mendel observed that desirable characteristics in peas could be encouraged through cross-breeding and then passed on to later generations of plants. From these experiments Mendel formulated his theory of genetics, and from this simple beginning the modern-day science of genetics has evolved.

In the years since Mendel conducted his experiments, tremendous advances have occurred in genetic science. The discovery of the DNA double helix in 1953 by Drs. Watson and Crick ushered in a revolution in science's comprehension of the nature, structure, and function of genes. Today science possesses an astounding comprehension of the genetic basis of life and its knowledge is increasing in exponential proportions.

Like Mendel, modern geneticists have sought ways to control genetic processes. With the discovery of restriction enzymes, scientists in the 1970's developed the ability through recombinant DNA techniques to identify, splice, and transfer genes in and between organisms. As a result of these developments, biotechnological achievements in industry, agriculture, and the health sciences have been phenomenal. New discoveries seem to be announced almost monthly.

As science has increased its gene-splicing abilities in other areas, it has simultaneously progressed toward the ultimate bio-

Excerpted from testimony by Congressman Albert Gore, Jr., of Tennessee before the House Subcommittee on Investigations and Oversight, 1982.

technology: human genetic engineering. Human genetic engineering was once thought to be impossible, the product of science fiction writers' vivid imaginations. Like so many other accomplishments in science and technology, however, human genetic engineering has moved from the realm of impossibility to certainty. The real question today thus is not whether human engineering will become a reality but, rather, when it will be so and for what purposes it will be used . . .

Again, it seems science has far outpaced expectations and predictions.

Recent developments

Recent developments in genetic research portend the imminence of human genetic engineering. Gene transplants have been successfully performed on laboratory animals, and the expectation is that these achievements will pave the way for similar transplants in humans. Moreover, one scientist actually attempted gene transplants on humans 2 years ago. The recent achievements in the labs will surely encourage new thoughts of human experimentation.

The potential development of the power to alter our genetic constitution gives us cause for both hope and concern. A number of diseases are known to be caused by gene defects, and it is said that these diseases could likely be cured through human gene therapy. However, these miraculous developments are not taking place in a vacuum. Other potential uses of this new science, such as the manipulation of physical traits and mental capacities, raise enormous questions of ethics, religion, and morality that our society must be prepared to confront. In many respects, we will be grappling with one of the most fundamental questions of all: What does it mean to be human? (Editor's Note: The chapters in this publication present **Ideas In Conflict** on the important moral and social issues raised by scientific developments in Genetic Engineering).

CHAPTER 1

HUMAN GENETIC ENGINEERING: THE SPLICE OF LIFE

THE SPLICE OF LIFE

WHOM DO WE DESIGNATE TO PLAY GOD?

Jeremy Rifkin

Jeremy Rifkin is the founder and director of the Foundation on Economic Trends (1346 Connecticut Avenue N.W., Suite 1010, Washington, D.C. 20036). He is the author of Algeny, *a critique of the emerging biotechnical society. His many speeches and articles warn of the moral and environmental dangers he thinks are presented by human genetic engineering.*

Points To Consider

1. How could genetic engineering change human life?
2. What is the difference between negative and positive eugenics?
3. Why is genetic engineering coming not as a threat but as a promise?
4. Why does genetic engineering represent the power of authorship over life?

Jeremy Rifkin, "Theological Letter Concerning the Moral Arguments Against Genetic Engineering of the Human Germline Cells," June, 1983.

Genetic engineering represents the power of authorship. Never before in history has such complete power over life been a possibility.

While the nation has begun to turn its attention to the dangers of nuclear war, little or no debate has taken place over the emergence of an entirely new technology which in time could very well pose as serious a threat to the existence of the human species as the bomb itself. We are referring to human genetic engineering. On July 22, 1982 the **New York Times** published a major editorial entitled "Whether to Make Perfect Humans." It will soon be possible, says the **Times**, to fundamentally alter the human species by engineering the genetic traits of the sex cells — the sperm and egg. Humanity's new found ability to engineer genetic traits could well lead to the creation of a new species, as different from homo-sapiens as we are to the higher apes. So grave is the threat of human genetic engineering that the **Times** suggests that we consider "the question of whether the human germline should be declared inviolable."

Programming genetic traits into human sex cells subjects the human species to the art of technological manipulation and architectural design.

With the arrival of human genetic engineering, humanity approaches a crossroads in its own technological history. It will soon be possible to engineer and produce human beings by the same technological design principles as we now employ in our industrial processes.

The wholesale design of human life, in accordance with technological prerequisites, design specifications, and quality controls, raises a fundamental question. Nobel laureate biologist Dr. Salvador Lauria puts the question in its most succinct context when he asks "When does a repaired or manufactured man stop being a man . . . and become a robot, an object, an industrial product?"

Nuclear Debate Similarities

The debate over genetic engineering is similar to the debate over nuclear power. For years the nuclear proponents argued that the potential benefits of nuclear power outweighed the potential harm. Today an increasingly skeptical public has begun to seriously question this basic presumption.

In a similar vein, proponents of human genetic engineering argue that the benefits outweigh the risks and that it would be irresponsible not to use this powerful new technology to elimi-

nate serious "genetic disorders." The **New York Times** editorial board correctly addressed this conventional scientific argument by concluding in its editorial that once the scientists are able to repair genetic defects "it will become much harder to argue against adding genes that confer desired qualities, like better health, looks or brains." According to the **Times,** "There is no discernible line to be drawn between making inheritable repairs of genetic defects, and improving the species."

Once we decide to begin the process of human genetic engineering, there is really no logical place to stop. If diabetes, sickle cell anemia, and cancer are to be cured by altering the genetic make-up of an individual, why not proceed to other "disorders:" myopia, color blindness, left handedness. Indeed, what is to preclude a society from deciding that a certain skin color is a disorder?

Engineering Extinction

The question, then, is whether or not humanity should "begin" the process of engineering future generations of human beings by technological design in the laboratory.

13

What is the price we pay for embarking on a course whose final goal is the "perfection" of the human species?

First there is the ecological price to consider. It is very likely that in attempting to "perfect" the human species we will succeed in engineering our own extinction. Eliminating so called "bad genes" will lead to a dangerous narrowing of diversity in the gene pool. Since part of the strength of our gene pool consists in its very diversity, including defective genes, tampering with it might ultimately lead to extinction of the human race. It should be recalled that in the 1950's genetic modifications were made in wheat strains to create bumper crops of "super wheat." When a new strain of disease hit the fields, farmers found that their wheat was too delicate to resist. Within two years, virtually the entire crop was destroyed.

Eugenics

Then there is the question of eugenics to carefully consider. Eugenics is the inseparable ethical wing of the Age of Biotechnology. First coined by Charles Darwin's cousin, Sir Francis Galton, eugenics is generally categorized into two types, negative and positive. Negative eugenics involves the systematic elimination of so-called biologically undesirable characteristics. Positive eugenics is concerned with the use of genetic manipulation to "improve" the characteristics of an organism or species . . .

The concern over a re-emergence of eugenics is well founded but misplaced. While professional ethicists watch out the front door for tell tale signs of a resurrection of the Nazi nightmare, eugenics doctrine has quietly slipped in the back door. The new eugenics is commercial not social. In place of the shrill eugenic cries for racial purity, the new commercial eugenics talks in pragmatic terms of medical benefits and improvement in the quality of life. The old eugenics was steeped in political ideology and motivated by fear and hate. The new eugenics is grounded in medical advance and the spectre of extending the human life span.

Genetic engineering, then, is coming to us not as a threat, but as a promise; not as a punishment but as a gift. And here is where the true danger lies. If the Brave New World comes, it will not be forced on us by an evil cabal of self-serving scientists and Machiavellian politicans. On the contrary, what makes opposition to the Brave New World so difficult is the seductive path that leads to it. Every new advance in human genetic engineering is likely to be heralded as a great stride forward, a boon for humankind. Every one of the breakthroughs in genetic engineering will be of benefit to someone, under some circumstance, somewhere in society. And step by step, advance by advance,

14

Awesome Power

The idea of imprisoning the life span of a human being by simply engineering its genetic blueprint at conception is truly awesome.

humans are no longer who we are

we human beings might well choose to trade away the spontaneity of natural life for the predictability of technological design until the human species as we know it is transformed into a product of our own creation; a product that bears only a faint resemblance to the original . . .

Ultimately, there is no security to be found in engineering the human species, just as we have now learned that there is no security to be found in building bigger, more sophisticated nuclear bombs.

Perhaps, if we had taken the time to look at the long range implications of our work in nuclear physics forty years ago, we might well have decided to restrict or prohibit the research and development of nuclear weaponry. Today we have the opportunity to look ahead and envision the final logical consequences of our work in genetic engineering. The question is whether we will choose to do so.

Just because something can be done is no longer an adequate justification for assuming it should be done or that it can't be stopped from being done. We believe we have a sacred obligation to say no when the pursuit of a specific technological path threatens the very existence of life itself.

Who Will Play God?

In deciding whether to go ahead or not with human genetic engineering we must all ask ourselves the following question. Who should we entrust with the authority to design the blueprints for the future of the human species? In the words of the Nobel laureate biologist George Wald, "Who is going to set those specifications?"

Human genetic engineering presents the human race with the most important political question it has ever had to contend with. Who do we entrust with the ultimate authority to decide which are the good genes that should be engineered into the human gene pool and which are the bad genes that should be eliminated?

15

Today the ultimate exercise of political power is within our grasp; the ability to control the future lives of human beings by engineering their characteristics in advance; making them a hostage of their own architecturally designed blueprints. Genetic engineering represents the power of authorship. Never before in history has such complete power over life been a possibility. The idea of imprisoning the life span of a human being by simply engineering its genetic blueprint at conception is truly awesome.

Aldous Huxley's spectre of a biologically designed caste system with its alphas, betas, gammas and deltas looms on the horizon. Our society must now ponder whether to give sanction to this fundamental departure in how human life is formed. In examining this issue, we would ask everyone to consider one simple question. Would we trust the Congress of the U.S. with the ultimate authority to decide which genes should be engineered into the human gene pool and which should be eliminated? Would we entrust the executive or judicial branch with such authority? Or the corporation and the marketplace? Or the scientists and the medical community?

Who do we designate to play God? The fact is, no individual, group, or set of institutions can legitimately claim the right or authority to make such decisions on behalf of the rest of the species alive today or for future generations.

Genetic engineering of the human germline cells represents a fundamental threat to the preservation of the human species as we know it, and should be opposed with the same courage and conviction as we now oppose the threat of nuclear extinction.

THE SPLICE OF LIFE

SOCIETY HAS NOTHING TO FEAR

Bernard D. Davis

Dr. Bernard Davis is a professor of bacterial physiology at the Harvard University Medical School, Boston, Massachusetts. In the following statement he argues that gene therapy and the whole question of genetic engineering present no threats to the human condition in the near future.

Points To Consider

1. What is wrong with the term "genetic engineering?"
2. What is meant by behavior modification?
3. How could genetic engineering be misused?
4. What is gene therapy and what promise does it offer to human life?

Excerpted from testimony by Bernard Davis before the House Subcommittee on Investigations and Oversight, 1982.

17

In the application of molecular genetics to man, where enormously beneficial results are appearing, I do not yet see any threats from which society needs protection.

The term "genetic engineering" is an unfortunate one, when applied to human beings. It carries overtones of a cold attitude toward people, as objects to be manipulated and remolded. Yet the goal of those working toward human applications of this technique is gene therapy—the replacement of the single defective genes that cause various hereditary diseases; and this aim is strictly within the humanitarian traditions of medicine. It is therefore essential, in discussing future prospects, to distinguish sharply between gene therapy and non-medical uses of genetic manipulation. The non-medical use that most people fear, of course, is the control of behavior for eugenic or political purposes.

Therapeutic and non-therapeutic applications not only differ in their aims: they also differ strikingly in the likelihood that we will have to deal with them in the foreseeable future, because they face very different technical problems. Unfortunately, however, most of the discussion of the subject has proceeded on the assumption that the two developments are indissolubly linked: if we developed the possibility of correcting the genetic cause of any disease we would also be creating the possibility of a Brave New World, with governments using the same techniques for deliberate interference with human nature.

This assumption became widely accepted when news of a spectacular scientific advance a dozen years ago, the isolation of a gene by Jonathan Beckwith and his colleagues, was accompanied by an even more newsworthy announcement: he regretted this success, because he believed that this line of research would soon lead to the power to manipulate human genes, and he did not trust our political system to ensure that this power would be used only to benefit the people. Quite apart from any preference for one or another political system, if I believed that we would indeed be reaching the capacity to use techniques of genetic modification to program human behavior in any general way I would also feel uneasy at that prospect, in the hands of any political system. But on purely technical grounds I disagree with the judgment that that power is in sight, or even is likely as far ahead as we can look. My reasons are the following.

First, the therapy even of single-gene defects is not yet around the corner, though replacement of defective cells is beginning to look feasible for those cells that function in widely

18

distributed, loosely organized locations. These include the precursor cells in the bone marrow that give rise to the red cells and the white cells of the blood, and the precursor cells that give rise to our specific immune responses. But even here there are still many technical obstacles to overcome.

When cells are arranged in a highly organized way, as in the liver or the kidney, the prospect of replacing them, or of introducing a desired gene into them in a reliably controlled way, is much dimmer.

Modifying Behavior

When we consider the technical problem of modifying behavior genetically we are dealing with an infinitely more complex pattern of cellular organization, involving a network of about 10 trillion specific connections between about 10 billion cells in the human brain. An enormous number of genes must be involved in the development of this circuitry, and any particular trait, such as intelligence or aggressiveness, must be influenced by a large number of these genes, interacting with each other and with the environment. It is therefore not suprising that we cannot yet identify a single specific behavioral gene, while we can identify several hundred that cause hereditary diseases.

Accordingly, the only prospect I can take seriously in this area, for the foreseeable future, would be a limited, vague alteration of behavior by influencing the level of various hormones. To achieve any more specific modification of behavior, involving altered circuitry, we would have to identify a set of genes that each have a small effect on a trait, isolate these genes, and transfer them together. Both the identification and the transfer would be very much more difficult than what we face with single-gene defects.

Another important difference is that behavior depends heavily on environmental influences as well as on genes. Accordingly, the effect of genetic changes on behavior would not be as sharply predictable as the effect of replacing an enzyme in a blood cell. An even greater obstacle arises from the difference in the time at which different genes act: most of the genes that contribute to individual differences in behavior must do so by guiding development of the intricate circuitry of the brain, and so they will have done their work before birth. And gene transfer could not conceivably rewire an already developed brain. In principle, one could circumvent this difficulty by replacing genes in germ cells. But this procedure would be useless, for one would be investing great effort to change some genes in a germ cell whose other genes were still an unknown, chance combination.

Finally, if some limited degree of genetic manipulation of behavior should ever become feasible, we must recognize that it would require cooperation of the subjects; and any population willing to cooperate in this way would already have lost its freedom. Moreover, this means of manipulating personalities would have to compete with other, less elaborate and less costly means, some already at hand. These include the familiar psychological methods, as well as possibilities provided by pharmacology, neurosurgery, and even eugenics (that is, selective breeding for the desired traits).

I cannot escape the conclusion that the rumors of the dangers of genetic blueprinting of behavior have been enormously exaggerated, and they have aroused much more public apprehension than the facts warrant. At the same time, it is clear that the development of effective gene therapy, even for a limited number of hereditary diseases, would be one of the greatest triumphs of medical science. And even if the procedure should prove to be expensive, its benefits would convert a miserable, helpless, and often brief life into a healthy one, and the costs would be amortized over that lifetime. This kind of research therefore deserves support and approval, rather than apprehension. It would be a tragedy if moral objections, based on fear of misuse of the same techniques, should interfere with such support and approval.

Cloning

I would now like to consider another type of genetic manipulation of humans that has seemed much closer than gene replacement: cloning. This creation of genetic copies of an individual has been successfully accomplished with frog embryos, by implanting nuclei from their body cells into egg cells. Ten years ago it seemed self-evident that improvements in technique would sooner or later extend the procedure to mammals, and also to the copying of tested adults rather than of undefined embryos. This scientific advance, if possible, would be of obvious value in agriculture, in the copying of prize animals.

The extension of cloning to man would raise such serious moral problems that I would oppose it. However, it now seems doubtful that we will have to face the problem. For while we know that all the different kinds of cells in our bodies contain essentially the same set of genes, recent work strongly suggests that as embryonic cells give rise to fully differentiated cells some of their genes change. Adult cells may therefore never be able to initiate clones. If this proves to be true the cloning of mammalian adults may well be unachievable, for fundamental reasons rather than for reasons that might be overcome by advances in technique. Human cloning by nuclear transplant, aimed at copying individuals with already demonstrated traits, would then lose its potential interest—and its threat.

Embryos, on the other hand, encounter no such problem as a source of clones. In fact, such cloning has already been accomplished in mice, not by nuclear transplantation but by separating the cells of a very early embryo and using each to start a new embryo. But while this procedure is indeed cloning, in the technical definition of the term, it is cloning of an unknown new individual rather than copying of a known. It is thus not a violation

'a new species'?

21

of our natural process of reproduction, which makes each individual unique by randomly recombining genes from the two parents; it is simply amplification of the process of producing identical twins. The motivation for this form of cloning is not nearly as obvious as that for cloning adults. I therefore do not see a problem that merits legislative attention now, though one might conceivably arise in the future.

Conclusion

Finally, we should note that molecular genetics has already made concrete contributions to medicine in a rapidly expanding area: prenatal diagnosis of hereditary defects. This development is of great benefit to those parents who both carry a recessive defect in the same gene: instead of accepting the 25% risk of a defective offspring, or also denying themselves children, for several diseases they now have the choice of solving the problem by prevention, even though it cannot yet be solved by gene therapy.

Let me close by emphasizing the need to protect the search for basic knowledge from being restricted by those who fear possible undesirable applications. All knowledge is double-edged; and we simply cannot foresee all the applications, and all the social consequences, of any discovery. We can serve society best not by blocking any particular knowledge but by better controlling its applications. In the physical sciences we have begun to resist certain applications that are too dangerous to people or damaging to the environment. If such applications appear in biology they should also be prohibited. But in the application of molecular genetics to man, where enormously beneficial results are appearing, I do not yet see any threats from which society needs protection.

MANIPULATING LIFE WILL TAKE PLACE

Stephen Stich

Dr. Stephen Stich is a professor of philosophy at the University of Maryland, College Park, Maryland. He is concerned about the moral and social problems posed by genetic engineering. He believes the western tradition of moral philosophy has left us unprepared to deal with the new human dilemmas presented by this revolutionary gene splicing technology.

Points To Consider

1. How does the author distinguish between somatic therapy and reproductive therapy?
2. What social problems could arise with genetic engineering?
3. Why has the western tradition of moral philosophy left us unprepared to deal with the dilemmas posed by genetic engineering?
4. What difficult decisions must humanity make?

Excerpted from testimony by Stephen Stich before the House Subcommittee on Investigations and Oversight, 1982.

***The western tradition of moral philosophy
has left us unprepared to deal with the
dilemmas posed by genetic engineering.***

intro

Humankind is embarked on an extraordinary adventure, an
adventure promising rewards that could barely have been imag-
ined as recently as a generation ago. But that adventure poses
moral and social dilemmas every bit as daunting as the rewards
are enticing. Moreover, some of those dilemmas are so unique,
so utterly unprecedented in human history that the tradition of
Western moral philosophy has left us quite unprepared to deal
with them. Within the moral and conceptual frameworks be-
queathed to us by our cultural tradition, we hardly know how to
begin thinking about some of the deeper problems posed by human genetic engineering.

Somatic Therapy

We have already seen the first tentative—some would say
premature—applications of recombinant DNA technology to humans. These efforts have been in the domain of so-called somatic therapy, aimed at correcting a genetic defect in cells or organs which are not involved in reproduction. If successful,
somatic therapy will alleviate the illness of the patient who re-
ceives the therapy, though he will still be a genetic carrier of the
disease, and will run the risk of passing his defective gene or
genes on to his offspring. There are many vexing questions
about the proper regulation of research on new somatic therapies. But, by and large, these issues are variations on a familiar
theme—the use of human subjects in medical research. I am inclined to think that the existing system for regulating and reviewing research involving human subjects can be extended to
research on somatic therapies with little difficulty.

Reproductive Therapy

A considerably more vexing cluster of problems arise when
our attention turns to therapeutic procedures which involve the
reproductive process. Typically, such procedures will be aimed
at subsequent generations, with the goal being to prevent a defective gene from being passed on from parent to child. As genetic therapy of this sort progresses, there is reason to hope that
such scourges as Tay-Sachs disease, Huntington's Chorea and
sickle cell disease will be all but wiped off the face of the Earth.

24

However, research in this domain will inevitably involve not only human sex cells but also human embryos and fetuses. Neither ethicists nor the society at large has reached any consensus about the moral propriety of such research or the rules under which it should be conducted. If we aim at a consistent, coherent set of moral principles, then there will be no separating the regulation of gene therapy research from the ongoing controversy over the morality of abortion, for in both cases the central issue to be confronted is the moral status of the human embryo.

Intense Social Pressures

As we learn more about the mechanisms of human genetics, it is inevitable that we will start learning how to manipulate the human genome to suit our tastes, or what we perceive to be our needs, in domains far removed from those that have traditionally been the concern of medicine.

At first this ability will be restricted to characteristics under the control of a single gene or a small number of genes. But, as our knowledge progresses, we will learn more and more about how to manipulate those characteristics of human beings—both physical and mental—which are under the control of many separate genes . . .

As our ability to manipulate the genetic composition of our own offspring grows in sophistication in the decades ahead, the social pressures to use this new technology will become intense.

During the last year or two we have seen an explosion of interest in home microcomputers; many of the people who buy these wonderful, expensive machines do so in the hope that they will give their children a competitive edge in a technologically competitive world. Closer to the fringes of our society we have seen that some women are prepared to have themselves impregnated with the sperm of a Nobel Prize winner in the hope of bearing an intellectually gifted child. Both of these phenomena underscore the fact that the desire to help one's children to excel is a powerful and widespread motivational force in our society. When, via genetic engineering we learn how to increase intelligence, memory, longevity, or other traits conveying a competitive advantage, it is clear that there will be no shortage of customers ready to take their place in line. Moreover, those who are unwilling or unable to take advantage of the new technology may find that their offspring have been condemned to a sort of second class citizenship in a world where what had been within the range of the normal gradually slips into the domain of the subnormal.

Social Problems

Now obviously if history unfolds more or less along the lines that I have been predicting, there will be no shortage of social problems generated. Insuring equitable access to the new technology and protecting the rights of parents and children who have chosen not to utilize the technology are two which come quickly to mind. These issues, however, are once again variations on a familiar theme. We already have analogous problems with equal access to high quality education for children. And in the decades ahead we will increasingly have to worry about the technological illiteracy of people from deprived educational backgrounds. I do not mean to suggest that these are unimportant concerns; far from it. Still, I am inclined to think that if problems of equity and discrimination were the only problems it generated, most people would welcome human genetic engineering as an almost unmixed blessing. Given the enormous increase in knowledge required to function in our increasingly technological society, it might well be argued that the capacity to improve our learning and reasoning abilities by genetic engineering had arrived just in the nick of time.

As we gradually map and learn to manipulate the human genome, however, it will become possible to alter or enhance many traits, not merely those, like intelligence and memory capacity, which are generally desirable and convey an obvious competitive advantage. We already know that many physical characteristics—height, build, color of the hair, eyes and skin, for

26

example—are in part determined by our genetic endowment. It is a good bet that tastes, character traits and other aspects of personality have a substantial genetic component as well. I do not think it is beyond the bounds of realistic possibility that in the next generation or two, and perhaps very much sooner, prospective parents will be able to choose from a library of genes in redesigning their own offspring. Nor is there any reason to suppose that all people or all societies will make the same choices. However, if different societies, or different groups within our own society make systematically different choices for several generations, we may begin to see the genetic fragmentation of the human species. The divisions that separate cultural groups may come to include genetic differences so profound that members of different groups will no longer be interfertile.

Western Tradition

I said earlier that the western tradition of moral philosophy has left us unprepared to deal with the dilemmas posed by genetic engineering. I would like now to spend a few moments expanding on that theme. Consider first the quandaries that arise when we try to think about such central ethical questions as the nature of the good or moral life, against the background of the emerging genetic engineering technology. From Socrates down to the present, just about everyone who has pondered the question of how men and women ought to live their lives has presupposed that human nature is in large measure fixed. There have, of course, been profound disagreements about what human nature is like. However, the moral issue has always been conceived of as attempting to determine what sort of life a person should lead, given that a human being is a certain sort of creature. This tradition leaves us radically unprepared to think about the questions forced upon us by the prospect of human genetic engineering. Sometime within the next century, and perhaps much sooner than that, the age old presumption of a more or less fixed human nature may begin to dissolve. It will no longer suffice to decide what constitutes the good or moral life for the sort of creature we happen to be; we shall also have to decide what sort of creature—or creatures—humankind ought to become. The options that human genetic engineering will make available are impossible to foresee in detail, though there is every reason to suspect that they will be numerous. No previous generation has had to give serious thought to such choices. Thus the moral and conceptual tools required to think about them will have to be invented as we go along . . .

In the western philosophical tradition there are many views about the nature of rational moral dialog and the quest for ethical agreement. But there is, I think, a common strand that runs through just about all theories on this subject. In one way or another, the notion of a shared human nature is rung in to explain how it is possible for people to reach a meeting of the minds on moral matters. When we are able to transcend our cultural and ideological differences, and agree on some ethical principle or judgment, it is because, despite our manifest differences, we share our humanity in common. Of course, our commonalities are all too often overwhelmed by our differences, and when this happens reason and dialog may give way to force. But at least our common nature gives us reason to hope that we share some common ground on which our attempts at rational persuasion can be built. However, human genetic engineering threatens to undermine the foundations of rational ethical dialog by fragmenting our common nature along social and ideological lines. How shall I reason with a Moslem fundamentalist or a Marxist or a Moonie if what divides him from me is not merely his traditions and his convictions, but also his genetics? The prospect is at once so staggering and so unprecedented that we hardly know how to begin thinking about it.

Conclusion

Let me close with some brief observations on the policy implications of these reflections. As I have already indicated, I think it would be a serious mistake to adopt policies aimed at preventing the development of a technology capable of making major modifications in the human genome. However, it is certainly an area that cries out for ongoing, informed monitoring. Thus I endorse with enthusiasm Professor Capron's proposal for an independent body, made up of scientists, ethicists, religious leaders, educators, and lay people whose function would not be to regulate, but to study issues as they appear on the horizon. Professor Capron stressed that education would be an important function of this body, and with this I also agree. However, I am inclined to urge a much stronger role for education in dealing with the challenge of genetic engineering and other new technologies. Unless the public and the political leaders who represent them come to have a better understanding of the basic science underlying these new technologies, there is little hope that our social decisions will be wise ones. This understanding does not come easy, and it will be expensive, but in the long run the distressingly low level of scientific understanding in our society will be more expensive still.

28

HUMAN GENETIC ENGINEERING IS IMPOSSIBLE

David Jackson

David Jackson is the vice president and chief scientific officer of Genex Corporation, Gaithersburg, Maryland. He feels that the public is overly concerned about the social and moral dangers of genetic engineering. He believes it will be impossible in the near future to genetically manipulate complex human traits.

Points To Consider

1. How is the genetic universe described?
2. What are the two classes of gene therapy?
3. How will gene therapy be used?
4. Why has the threat of human genetic engineering been blown out of proportion?

Excerpted from testimony by David Jackson before the House Subcommittee on Investigations and Oversight, 1982.

The idea that it will be possible to successfully and directly engineer complex human traits in any foreseeable future is simply preposterous.

Genetic engineering is a term which has gained great currency during the past 10 years, yet in spite of that, I think there is surprisingly little consensus about what it means, particularly in an operational sense. It is certainly true that enormous progress has been made in our ability to manipulate some genes in some genetic contexts very precisely. It is equally true that many of the widely discussed applications of genetic engineering, especially many of the ones involving applications to humans, are of almost unimaginable complexity. They certainly cannot be done now. Moreover, it is unclear that they will be possible, let alone desirable from either a pragmatic or an ethical perspective, in the clearly foreseeable future.

Genetic engineering involves working with DNA molecules. DNA molecules are of central importance in all living organisms where they perform two principal functions. Both functions depend on the fact that the entire heritable information of an organism—all of its genes—is stored in a kind of code in its DNA molecules. The first function of DNA is to transmit all of this information to the next generation of the organism, which the DNA does by duplicating itself and distributing identical copies to the progeny cells. The second function of DNA is to serve as the data base which is used to program all of the thousands of chemical reactions which must occur in living cells.

The Genetic Universe

DNA molecules are long, stringlike molecules made up of only four different kinds of building blocks called A, C, G, and T. All the information stored in the DNA is contained in the sequence in which these four building blocks occur along the molecule. That is, the language of DNA is written with a four-letter alphabet. The sequence of building blocks in the DNA is converted into a sequence of similar building blocks in a related type of molecule called messenger RNA. The sequence of building blocks in the messenger RNA is in turn used to program the cellular machinery which makes enzymes or proteins. Enzymes are protein molecules which act as specific catalysts for the thousands of chemical reactions which occur in living cells.

In simple terms, a gene is that segment of a DNA molecule which codes for a single type of enzyme molecule. An average

gene contains 1,500 to 2,000 of the building blocks. Even the simplest living organisms contain several thousand genes this size. The cells of the most complex organisms, such as man, contain approximately 1,000 times as much DNA as those of simple organisms such as bacteria. Another way of saying this is that if a typical gene is around 1,500 building blocks in length, then the simplest living organisms contain about 3 million building blocks' worth of DNA—all of it is in a single molecule composed only of A, G, C, and T—and the most complex organisms have about 3 billion building blocks in their DNA.

The complexity of this genetic material can be graphically appreciated by thinking of the DNA molecule as a piece of yarn, in which the yarn is about 100,000 times the size of the DNA molecule. On this scale, a typical gene is just over 2 inches long. On this same scale, the DNA content of the simplest microorganisms is about one-tenth of a mile of yarn. And the DNA content of a single human cell is equivalent to about 100 miles of yarn. To appreciate the genetic complexity of human DNA, imagine walking from Washington to Baltimore and back and seeing 15 to 20 new genes every step of the way, each one composed of about 1,500 building blocks smaller than the size of a period on a printed page.

I have emphasized the extraordinary genetic complexity of human DNA because that complexity, in and of itself, places several limits on what one could hope to accomplish with human genetic engineering.

Two Classes of Genetic Engineering

As Professor Capron indicated, when one comes to a question of gene therapy, there are basically two classes of genetic engineering involving introduction of foreign DNA molecules into human cells to be considered.

These are what you referred to as the somatic and the germline approach. The first involves inserting "good" copies of a gene which is defective into a human embryo at an extremely early stage of development. Leaving aside the formidable problems of how to identify an embryo carrying a defective gene at such an early stage of development, I find it almost impossible to believe that the precision with which we can engineer something as complex as the DNA of human cells will be attained with a sufficiently high level of confidence that the procedure will be either ethically acceptable or pragmatically desirable. Recall that many genetic diseases are caused by a single incorrect building block out of the 3 billion or so in each cell.

The second type of genetic engineering involves attempting to cure individuals who have been diagnosed as having a genetic disease by some form of gene therapy. Here, too, there are formidable technical problems. In order to begin to work on a gene therapy approach to curing a genetic disease, the nature of the biochemical defect must in general be known.

Even if a good copy of the defective gene is in hand, there are major problems in introducing it into the target tissue, let alone to an adequate site inside the target cell where the disease is manifest. The major exception to this statement is genetic diseases of the blood, one of the few organs of the body which can be easily removed, manipulated in the laboratory at the cellular level and then reintroduced into the body. I wish to emphasize that in the foreseeable future genetic engineering is likely to require manipulation of human cells in the laboratory. It is possible that gene therapy may be developed for a few diseases of the blood, such as sickle cell anemia and thalassemia, during the next several decades. It is unlikely that similar success will be achieved for genetic diseases affecting other organs of the body.

In spite of the generally bleak picture for gene therapy as a treatment for human genetic diseases, there are extremely promising and much less controversial ways in which genetic engineering is being successfully used to treat genetic diseases

32

today. This approach is to use genetically engineered bacteria to synthesize the active human protein which is lacking in the individual afflicted with the genetic diseases. This approach has already been successfully applied to the treatment of congenital dwarfism and diabetes with the synthesis of human growth hormone and human insulin in genetically engineered bacteria. Additional human proteins with proven therapeutic potential for other genetic diseases are being developed in a variety of labs at the present time.

Conclusion

I wish to make one other point about the application of genetic engineering to human beings. A great deal of popular literature is based on the premise that it will soon be possible to use genetic engineering for directed manipulation—that is to say, manipulation where a predetermined result is sought and achieved—of complex characteristics such as intelligence, aggressiveness, personality, good looks, and so forth. All of these characteristics, to the extent that their determinants are genetic, are surely specified by many genes, none of which do we have the slightest clue at the present time as to how to identify biochemically. The idea that it will be possible to successfully and directly engineer such complex human traits in any foreseeable future is simply preposterous.

33

INTERPRETING EDITORIAL CARTOONS

This activity may be used as an individualized study guide for students in libraries and resource centers or as a discussion catalyst in small group and classroom discussions.

Although cartoons are usually humorous, the main intent of most political cartoonists is not to entertain. Cartoons express serious social comment about important issues. Using graphic and visual arts, the cartoonist expresses opinions and attitudes. By employing an entertaining and often light-hearted visual format, cartoonists may have as much or more impact on national and world issues as editorial and syndicated columnists.

Points to consider

1. Examine the cartoon in this activity.
2. How would you describe the cartoon's message?
3. Try to summarize the message in one to three sentences.
4. Does the cartoon's message support the author's point of view in any of the opinions in chapter one of this book? If the answer is yes, be specific about which reading or readings and why.

New bug

Reprinted by permission from *The Minneapolis Star and Tribune.*

34

CHAPTER 2

CONFLICTING HUMAN VALUES: RELEASING THE GENETIC GENIE

ENORMOUS POTENTIAL FOR GOOD

Alexander Capron

*Alexander Morgan Capron recently completed three years'
service as executive director of the President's
Commission for the Study of Ethical Problems in Medicine
and Biomedical and Behavioral Research, which rendered
its final report early in 1983. He is currently a professor of
law, ethics, and public policy at Georgetown University.*

Points to Consider

1. How is the term "genetic engineering" defined?
2. What are the medical applications of genetic engineering?
3. How is the "Frankenstein Factor" described and what is its relationship to genetic engineering?
4. What potential benefits does gene therapy offer humankind?

Alexander Capron, "Enormous Potential for Good,", **Imprimis,** June,
1983, pp. 1–4. Reprinted by permission from **Imprimis,** the monthly
journal of Hillsdale College, featuring presentations at Hillsdale's Center
for Constructive Alternatives and its Shavano Institute for National
Leadership.

To expect humanity to turn its back on what may be one of the greatest technological revolutions may itself betray a failure to recognize the limits of individual and social self-restraint.

In 1965 the term "genetic engineering" was coined for what has come to be a wide range of techniques by which scientists can add genetically determined characteristics to cells that would not otherwise have possessed them . . .

In the early 1970s, scientists learned how to isolate specific sequences in the deoxyribonucleic acid (or DNA) from one species and attach this genetic material—"recombinant DNA"—to a different species. The layperson's term "gene splicing" describes the technology well, for like a seaman putting two pieces of rope together, a scientist using the recombinant DNA method can chemically "snip" a DNA chain at a predetermined place and attach another piece of DNA at that site.

My conclusion is that the technique is one with enormous potential for good—but we must look before we leap. There is need for public participation in an explicit process of scrutinizing the ethical and social implications of gene splicing . . .

Today it is apparent that gene splicing has many practical applications—in industry, in agriculture and in medicine. I want to concentrate on the latter—to provide a focus for our discussion because I think it is the application that raises the most interesting questions.

Medical Applications

The President's Commission has recently completed a study of the medical applications of genetic engineering. We examined three ways in which gene splicing may enter into the treatment of human beings. Moving from the most near-at-hand and familiar to the most far-off and controversial, they are: the production of useful drugs and biologics, the diagnosis of genetic diseases and the cure of such diseases.

You have probably already heard about the first of these subjects, particularly the use of recombinant DNA techniques to create bacteria capable of producing desirable medical products—like interferon or human growth hormone.

The second area in which gene splicing can be applied in medical care—namely in genetic screening and diagnosis—has also recently begun bearing fruit. This technique holds great promise for genetic disorders that until now have not been readily diagnosable . . .

The most novel and important area is in using gene splicing to cure genetic disorders. If this proves possible, it would differ from other treatments because it would not involve the manipulation of the patient or the application (often continually) of a drug but the actual alteration of the cause of the condition itself . . .

The Frankenstein Factor

In reviewing statements about gene splicing in the popular press, I have been struck by the frequent invocation of what Willard Gaylin some years ago called the "Frankenstein factor." The analogy is illuminating for several reasons. First, Dr. Frankenstein was a creator of new life and the gene splicers have raised questions about mankind's role as creator. Second, Dr. Frankenstein's creation was a frightening monster and gene splicing has raised fears about strange new life forms . . .

The Frankenstein analogy bespeaks people's concern that something is being done to them and their world by individuals concerned with their own goals but not necessarily with human betterment. As C.S. Lewis once observed, "Man's power over

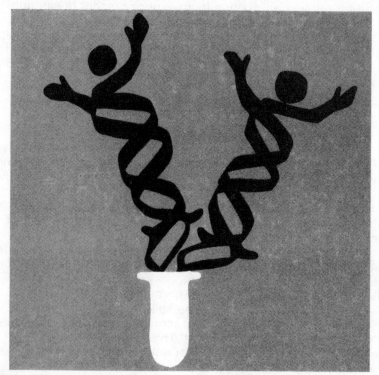

nature is really the power of some men over others with nature as their instrument."

But most particularly, it seems to me that the Frankenstein story was on the lips of many people—both scientists and lay people—because it dealt with the creation of a new being with a human form.

Like the new knowledge associated with Copernicus, Darwin, Freud, and Einstein, that associated with the gene splicers offers further challenge to human beings' conception of themselves as the unique center of the universe. By identifying DNA and learning how to manipulate it, science seems to have reduced people to a set of malleable molecules that can be interchanged with those of species that people regard as inferior.

And unlike the earlier revolutionary discoveries, those in molecular biology are not merely descriptive; they give scientists vast new power for action. The use of this new power has frequently been labelled "playing God." This description carries with it an implication that it is wrong for human beings to engage in this activity at all—that we have overreached ourselves by pretending to have God-like powers.

This objection has several possible meanings. At least one is not persuasive. For millenia, people have interfered with nature both intentionally and unintentionally as a side effect of other human activities. There is some difference in aspects of gene splicing, however, that might create hybrids that are capable of reproducing themselves—but here the concern would not be that crossing species lines is inherently wrong, merely that if the effects are deleterious their harm may be multiplied by their perpetuation into later generations—like a recombinant DNA Dutch elm disease. This is an issue that deserves to be treated with great care, but it is not one that raises a problem of principle.

There is, however, another aspect to the complaint about "playing God" in crossing species lines where a prohibition may be in order, and that is in the hybridization of human beings with other living things.

The prospect of creating an actual being with partially human characteristics offends a deeply held taboo. There is, however, no legal or regulatory prohibition of such a step. And if the barrier is to survive in the face of scientific advances, the reasoning behind it will need further attention. It may, for example, be fruitful to clarify what it is about human beings that is unique—whether it is the sum of their characteristics or the possession of particular characteristics. There is a certain irony here since a person approaching the subject from a religious or philosophical position is likely to deny that human beings are simply a reflection of the particular chemicals that make them up, and yet the objection being raised is to an alteration in those chemicals.

The Genetic Revolution

The genetic revolution in medicine has begun. Its goal is the overthrow of tyrants that long have plagued the human race: cancer, heart disease, birth defects and other ills.

Scientists are working on genetic ways to correct inherited flaws and find the causes of diseases, improve diagnoses, monitor treatment and achieve cures.

Gordon Slovut and Lewis Cape, *Minneapolis Tribune*, 1983

When one moves from absolute prohibitions on the human uses of gene splicing to questions of particular consequences, one is faced immediately with a realization of the great uncertainty in this field.

The concern for personal health has several bases. One is the notion that in replacing a particular DNA sequence that is regarded as deleterious, a physician might also unintentionally be removing other genetic material that is in fact beneficial. Moreover, even when only a particular gene is replaced there is a risk that some advantage supplied by the gene may be lost. Little is known about the range of effects a single gene can have; many affect several parts of the body in what appears to be a wide variety of ways.

The possibility that genetic changes would be inherited also raises many questions. For example, would such alternations be so widespread in society that the gene pool would lose desirable diversity, thereby exposing mankind—like some inbred strain of rice or corn—to the risk of decimation by a newly arising pathogen?

Social Questions

In addition, the ability to change one's genes challenges the basic assumptions about people's links to, and responsibility for, their progeny. In some ways, one's responsibility may be increased: Will it be acceptable for people simply to take the results of the natural lottery by which characteristics are now determined, or will responsible parents be expected to "correct" bad genes and to augment others to give their children an opportunity for a higher level of physical or cognitive functioning?

On the other hand, knowing that future generations may em-

40

ploy an even more advanced technology to alter or to replace characteristics passed on to them may weaken people's sense of genetic continuity. Furthermore, by blurring the line between what counts as a serious defect or disability and what is "normal functioning," gene splicing may alter our perception of what society owes to children, particularly those burdened by handicaps.

The potential of gene therapy or surgery to improve functioning calls into question the scope and limits of a central element of a democratic political theory: the commitment of equality of opportunity. Would genetic engineering become mandatory— along, perhaps, with restrictions on natural reproduction—in order to avoid the effects of the natural lottery that has such a profound influence on our opportunities in life?

Any discussion of equality leads naturally into a discussion of justice. Who should decide which line of genetic engineering ought to be pursued and which applications of the technology to which patients ought to be undertaken? This is a question that seldom arises about medical progress. Decisionmaking in medicine is widely dispersed, resting upon the tripod of peer standards, patient consent, and very broad and general state regulation. But if genetic engineering comes to be seen as a very beneficial and powerful form of treatment, questions will certainly be raised about access to it not only in the use of techniques that have been developed but also in deciding about which areas need to be pursued . . .

Even after the potential consequences have been carefully sifted and their implications for human welfare have been explored, there remains an important residual concern expressed by the warning against "playing God." It reminds human beings that they are only human and will some day have to pay if they underestimate their own ignorance and fallibility.

At this point in the development of genetic engineering no reasons have been found for abandoning the entire enterprise— indeed, it would probably be naive to assume that it could be. To expect humanity to turn its back on what may be one of the greatest technological revolutions may itself betray a failure to recognize the limits of individual and social self-restraint.

Assuming that research will continue somewhere, it seems more prudent to encourage its development and control under the sophisticated and responsive regulatory arrangements of this country, subject to the scrutiny of a free press and within the general framework of democratic institutions.

WE DO NOT HAVE THE WISDOM

Liebe Cavalieri

Liebe F. Cavalieri is a professor of biochemistry at the Graduate School of Medical Sciences, Cornell University. He has also had a long association with the Sloan-Kettering Institute for Cancer Research. As a researcher, he is credited with pioneering discoveries in the molecular biology of DNA. As a science writer, his publications include the book The Double-Edged Helix: Science in the Real World.

Points to Consider

1. How is genetic engineering compared with nuclear fission?
2. What are society's most serious problems and why will genetic engineering not offer a "quick fix?"
3. Why is it foolish to think man can improve on the design of nature?
4. What is the danger of gene therapy?

Liebe Cavalieri, "We Do Not Have the Wisdom," **Imprimis,** June, 1983, pp. 4–6. Reprinted by permission from **Imprimis,** the monthly journal of Hillsdale College, featuring presentations at Hillsdale's Center for Constructive Alternatives and its Shavano Institute for National Leadership.

In the face of the infinite complexity of natural systems, the idea that we could improve on the design of nature is not only hubris, it is frightening.

The very core of life has been put at man's disposal. What had been a scholarly, reflective science, molecular biology, was transformed, ten years ago, into a force that not only can examine the living organism but now can manipulate it in ways never before possible, at the will of the scientist.

Life systems can be restructured by creating a new architecture for DNA. Living cells of all types can be engineered so that they can perform tasks foreign to their species. Bacteria can be transformed so that they carry out human functions. Cancer viruses can be propagated inside bacteria. Mice can be grown to twice their normal size. Intervention in the germ line (reproductive cells) of mice has been achieved, opening the way for similar procedures in humans.

We can anticipate that recombinant DNA technology will present problems that are as pervasive and disquieting as those that have sprung from nuclear fission. Both are major scientific accomplishments that confer a power on humans for which they are psychologically and morally unprepared. The physicists have already learned this, to their dismay; the biologists, not yet.

Nobel laureate David Baltimore has recently proclaimed: "We can outdo evolution"—a signal that molecular biologists are about to translate genetic engineering into an instrument of power, much the way the physicists did when they exploited their discoveries at the beginning of the nuclear age.

Economic Demands vs. Human Needs

In the habitual manner of our times, scientists are pursuing their interests and then rationalizing the pursuit by looking for uses for their discoveries, whether society needs them or not, rather than starting with the most pressing problems and looking for solutions. This may have been acceptable in the past but I'm not sure society can afford this luxury right now, when it is facing an alarming series of threats that have recently become apparent.

These threats include water and air pollution by industrial products and wastes, accelerating soil erosion and desertification, exhaustion of renewable resources such as water and forests faster than they can be replenished, the "greenhouse" effect, acid rain, ozone depletion, species extinction, depletion of mineral resources, excessive population growth, malnutrition—not to mention the nuclear arms race.

These are not separate problems; all are interrelated, and in the long run they are exacerbated by the fact that solutions are sought on an individual basis, with no regard for the consequences that any given "solution" might have for other members of the set. Too often, economic demands are pitted against human needs.

Recombinant DNA technology has been so widely promoted by scientists and the news media that industrial giants from all over the world have been induced to invest heavily in it. Genetic manipulation of micro-organisms by the new techniques has proceeded rapidly and is now widespread. More than 150 genetic engineering firms mainly oriented just now toward the design of industrially useful micro-organisms, have formed in the last few years. The technology has been translated into economic power, and with it molecular biologists have become entrepreneurs, leaving the Ivory Tower far behind.

The profound ecological, social, and ethical implications of genetic engineering have been obscured by its marketability. All forms of life are vulnerable to this technology—any DNA can be connected to any other DNA; human DNA can be put into viruses and bacteria and vice versa; cancer virus DNA has already been put into bacteria, and so on. The gene pool of the Earth, the life-determinant of the future, is the experimental subject for genetic engineering. This precious, irreplaceable legacy of natural evolution is in the truest sense a one-time occurrence, and it would be naive to assume that we can manipulate it without harming ourselves. We do not have the requisite infinite wisdom.

Delicate Mechanism

In the face of the infinite complexity of natural systems, the idea that we could improve on the design of nature is not only hubris, it is frightening. In Lewis Thomas's words, we are ignorant "most of all about the enormous, imponderable system of life in which we are embedded as working parts. We do not really understand nature at all." We know that the Earth behaves like an indivisible, delicately tuned mechanism, in which the inanimate environment is strongly conditioned by living things, and vice versa; but we have only begun to decipher the influence of each part on the whole . . .

However, as the result of current efforts to design industrially useful organisms, micro-organisms with properties taken from higher forms of life will inevitably escape into the ecosphere;

other engineered forms will eventually be released intentionally into the environment for purposes such as the digestion of oil spills. We are laying the groundwork for unforeseen evolutionary changes that may create an environment inhospitable to present species.

Frequently, one is confronted with specious arguments about how well evolutionary forces have managed thus far and how they will continue to provide viable ecosystems. Certainly, we can find some assurance in nature's resiliency; life has survived environmental upheavals for millions of years. But as conditions have changed, so has the balance of life, with incompatible forms disappearing and new ones arising. If there were a drastic change in the environment, some forms of life would undoubtedly adapt, but humans, with their many, exacting biological requirements, could not evolve fast enough to become compatible with the new environment.

Genetic engineers have many visions. They plan to introduce foreign genes into crop plants in the hope of solving the problem of world hunger. But food experts and agronomists recognize that enough is already produced to feed everyone in the world. Distribution is the problem; it is not scientific but rather economic and political.

It is obvious that it would be naive to attempt to solve the food problem with recombinant DNA technology. Even if that technology should someday succeed in producing plants that can fix atmospheric nitrogen, the most that could be hoped for would be a small contribution of a temporary respite—a technological fix that has no bearing on the fundamental population problem and might have adverse side effects that would exacerbate the situation by producing ecological instability.

Bacterias that will consume oil from oil spills on the oceans have already been produced. In addition to ecological questions, the social implications of this procedure are far-reaching. It has been shown that crude oil spilled from faulty tankers has an adverse effect on marine life. The application of vast numbers of bacteria to consume the spill would doubtlessly lead to mutant forms with an altered metabolism, so that some might find a niche in the oceans or even on land, causing ecological disturbances.

'When Do We Start?'

Genetic engineers have not overlooked the possibility of changing man himself. It will not be long before single-gene replacement therapy—the correction of a defective gene—will be possible. Although in this case the change will die with the patient, more radical experiments are underway in which eggs or sperm are altered to produce individuals with hereditary alterations. Considerable success along these lines has already been achieved in mice.

The rationale for these experiments is that they provide information about mammalian genetics and fetal development. But when the technology for intervention in human evolution has been perfected, will it remain unused? Preliminary experiments with human embryos have been underway in England, for example, for several years. What is more seductive than the power to design human beings?

Although the repair of genetic defects appears laudable, the indistinct boundary between repair and improvement raises serious problems. Who is to decide what qualities define a perfect human? In a changing world, the genetic engineering of perfection would imply a divine intelligence that could peer far into the future. There are some scientists who think they have such power. Professor James Bonner of Cal Tech has recently suggested:

The logical outcome of activities in modifying the genetic make-up of man is to reach the stage where couples will want their children to have the best possible genes. Sexual procreation will be virtually ended. One suggestion has been to remove genetic material from each individual immediately after birth and then promptly sterilize that individual. During the individual's lifetime, records would be kept of accomplishments and characteristics. After the individual's death, a committee decides if the accomplishments are worthy of procreation into other individuals. If so, genetic material would be removed from the depository and stimulated to clone a new individual. If the committee decides the genetic material is unworthy of procreation it is destroyed . . . The question is indeed not a moral one but a temporal one—when do we start?

Such men have fallen into the trap that often stands between scientists and the realization of a mature social conscience: reductionism, the operational form of modern scientific research. It requires that the system under investigation be first separated

46

into its most minute components. The forest as a whole may thereby pass unnoticed.

This is a common pattern in our society. The focus is on specific and immediate problems, considered individually and in isolation from life as a whole. It is inevitable under these circumstances that the chosen solution to one problem will exacerbate another. Long-range social and economic well-being can never be attained by systematically ignoring the interrelatedness of our problems and the side effects and more distant consequences of our decisions; this fragmented approach is condemning us to crisis after crisis.

The Core of Life

The Global 2000 Report to the President, which appeared in 1980, is a stark testimony to this. The report projects that if we continue on the same path, "the world in the year 2000 will be more crowded, more polluted, less stable ecologically, and more vulnerable to disruption than the world we live in now. Despite greater material output, the world's people will be poorer in many ways than they are today." The report calls for "new initiatives, if worsening poverty, human suffering, environmental degradation and international tension and conflicts are to be prevented. There are no quick fixes. New and imaginative ideas—and a willingness to act on them—are essential."

Insofar as the scientific community has been distinguished by the purity of its motivation and its lack of bias and self-interest, to that same extent it has been free of corrupting power. But today power is thrust upon the scientist by the comprehensive knowledge he has gained, as well as by the vast technological influence of science in our society. To be true to itself, science must reject power in favor of responsibilty. The scientist must have a conscience. Hand wringing after the fact offers no solution, as we have learned from the nuclear experience.

The discoveries that energy can be released from the atomic nucleus and that DNA, the material of the cell nucleus, is the genetic stuff of life are without parallel in human experience. These twin scientific feats, one at the core of matter, the other at the core of life, demand a new consciousness if human life on this planet is to continue.

We have mismanaged the applications of the first discovery. Now, as the second is about to be exploited, we must not permit the biosphere, surpassing as it does our understanding, to become an experimental subject. There is only one Earth, one earthly biosphere, and we are part of it. There is no margin for error.

A BIBLICAL VIEW OF GENETIC ENGINEERING

Wes Granberg-Michaelson

Wes Granberg-Michaelson, a Sojourners *contributing editor, is a member of Community Covenant Church in Missoula, Montana, and executive director of the recently founded New Creation Institute. He is a former managing editor of* Sojourners *magazine.*

Points to Consider

1. Why is "life itself" being commercialized?
2. What are the most alarming features of the biotechnology revolution?
3. Why has the church's response to the genetic revolution been inadequate?
4. What is biotechnology and what does it intend to do?
5. Why is humanity not prepared for the new powers of genetic engineering?

From Auschwitz to Hiroshima to Love Canal, humanity has decisively demonstrated that its technological powers overwhelm its capacities for moral judgment. The genetic engineering of human life, if allowed to proceed, will quickly trespass any well-intentioned boundaries and guidelines.

The desire to be like God, while present since the fall, is becoming a technological possibility. The publisher of U.S. News and World Report introduced a recent cover article on biotechnology by writing:

No longer do [scientists] have to wait for nature to provide the combination of genetic traits they want in microbes, plants, animals—even human beings. They can simply splice new genes into cells to create the organisms they want.

While the church's stand against humanity's nuclear ability to destroy created life becomes more steadfast each day, its response to the technological ability to create new life has been weak, ambiguous, and muted. Yet equally profound dangers are present. Further, central theological judgments about the integrity of life are being made by researchers in universities and corporations, largely unnoticed by the church.

An unprecedented ability to create and manufacture new forms of life has emerged in scientific laboratories. In 1980, the U.S. Supreme Court ruled that new forms of genetically engineered life could be granted patents. Within two years, more than 150 genetic engineering firms were established, many with the enthusiastic backing and capital of Wall Street . . .

Commercializing Life

A startling occurrence is happening here. As life itself is commercialized, it is defined only according to its material characteristics. The vital, sacred, and reverential qualities of life evaporate away. We are left simply with a vast new pool of "material" to be technologically manipulated into forms of economic utility.

Dr. Leon Kass, a molecular biologist and author, sees it this way:

We have paid some high prices for the technological conquest of nature, but none perhaps so high as the intellectual and spiritual costs of seeing nature as mere material for our manipulation, exploitation, and transformation. With the powers for bio-

logical engineering now gathering, there will be splendid new opportunities for a similar degradation of our view of man [sic].

The future possibilities of the bio-engineering of life are being set neither by moral or theological judgments, nor by governmental guidelines, but simply by economic feasibilities. The bio-chip seems destined to replace the microchip as the technological icon of a new age. Humanity now has the power to recreate the fabric of life, including the life of the human species. As with nuclear power, the consequences of this capacity are awesome, and without precedent in human history.

Meanwhile, society's technological euphoria over genetic engineering has smothered the already faint theological and moral qualms. Cover stories in Time and Newsweek, as well as coverage on television newscasts, all stress the amazing prospects for rescuing the U.S. economy, solving the energy crisis, and revolutionizing agriculture that genetic engineering could bring. Such media coverage echoes the hope of stories in 1945 and 1946 describing how the harnessing of nuclear power would revolutionize transportation, make energy limitless, and even control the weather.

Society's hope for a technological fix for its economic, environmental, and resource problems now rests on genetic engineering. The root causes of economic stagnation, ecological deterioration, and resource scarcity can all be avoided by believing that genetic engineering will provide a purely technical solution. . . .

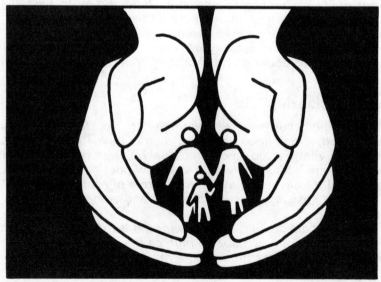

Church's Response

What, then, should be the church's response to the dramatic unfolding of genetic engineering?

First, the biblical directive to care for creation assumes a relationship of cooperation and involvement with the created world. Arguing against interfering with the "natural order" misses the point. Humanity's life is never separate from the rest of creation, but intrinsically tied to it. The instructions of Genesis 2 to till and keep the garden, and numerous Old Testament admonitions to care for the land, call us to a stance of caretaking, rather than exploiting, the creation. Ownership is the central question. The Bible declares that creation is God's, and not ours.

Wearing eyeglasses, growing tomatoes, taking aspirin, and eating three meals a day all involve some attempt to affect the natural order. Genetic engineering begins in its mildest forms as another such attempt. Some of its results, such as inexpensive insulin, improved treatment of burns, and various vaccines may indeed be beneficial in the short run.

Rather than issuing abstract warnings against any tampering with nature, the church should examine how various possibilities of genetic engineering affect the relationship between humanity, creation, and God. Practitioners of genetic engineering, however, have generally been suspicious of moral, ethical, and theological discussion of their activities. They often stand behind a classic defense of scientific inquiry. Society, and especially religion, the practitioners say, should not and must not attempt to limit the scope of scientific investigation.

But the matter is not that simple. In unique ways, genetic engineering welds together science and technology with immediate effects on nature. New variations and forms of life are created and potentially introduced into the eco-system. This is not free inquiry; it is the creation of new facts and new relationships in the world of nature.

Similarly, proponents of biotechnology often declare that one cannot stand in the way of scientific and technological progress. If something can be done, then it should be done, and will be done anyway, regardless of reservations. But this only admits a slavery to the technological process.

It is foolhardy to do everything that technology allows us to do. The progress of genetic engineering, in fact, should make this self-evident.

Historically the impetus for pushing any technology to the extremes of potential human destructiveness has come from the military. Today, we can assume that in some top-secret laboratories and think tanks in our land, people are researching how the tools and potential creations of genetic engineering could be used against the nation's enemies.

Since General Electric has now patented a micro-organism that can eat up the oil from a tanker spill, why not develop a strategy for unleashing it in the Soviet Union's oil fields? Why not create a micro-organism capable of carrying behavior-modifying drugs, in an undetectable manner, to Soviet military personnel and strategic planners? What about a new microbe that would rust Nicaragua's military equipment in just a few days?

Why not cross human genes with an animal and breed a new organism not quite human, programed with a biochip to carry out military instructions unto death? And shouldn't there be a small number of genetically engineered humans with super-intelligence, raised under careful military supervision and devoted to spending their lives thinking of strategies to outwit the nation's enemies?

We can assume that bizarre possibilities like these are being contemplated and evaluated as part of military research. Once society uncritically blesses the advance of genetic engineering, its manipulation for military purposes accelerates without restraint. Eventually, as with nuclear power, it will become difficult to separate military applications from civilian uses. The church should sound the warning to these dangers.

Public developments in genetic engineering are being driven by their profit-making potential. Here again as with nuclear power, the hope of economic returns discounts the inherent risks in the technology. The immediate, short-run benefits which seem humane and undeniable are embraced, while the long-term dangers posed to the genetic and ecological balance of life are ignored . . .

Biotechnology

Biotechnology has no intention of stopping with the creation of a few new commercially useful microbes. Rapidly, it is moving up the scale of life, even developing the ability to create whole new species. Far more than simply breeding hybrids is involved.

In 1981, scientists successfully transfered a rabbit gene into a mouse embryo, and the newborn mouse (with a little bit of rabbit) successfully mated. Reprograming a whole species became possible, transferring distinct traits of one animal to another. The corporations that produce modified species could claim a patent and ownership on every such modified beast that was ever born. The Supreme Court's 1980 decision opening the way for corporations to patent new life forms reflects how deeply society believes that creation is ours to possess.

The point, of course, is not whether animals should serve humans. Modifying and nurturing animal breeds as well as plant varieties has long been done. But genetic engineering presents wholly novel possibilities. One species can now be altered with traits of another. Species boundaries are no longer inviolate, but can be crossed at will. New species of life can be brought into existence, all to satisfy economic whims.

Instead of seeing a given species as an established and purposeful part of creation's order, the genetic engineer sees simply a genetic program at work. That program can be modified, reworked, and altered in any way deemed useful. The life of a species compels no inherent respect. It is merely a particular programing of information.

What would be the likely consequences if humanity so controlled and dominated the variation of species? The bald eagle, rainbow trout, grizzly bear, and lady bug would have no intrinsic value. Their worth would depend only on their commercial, recreational, or aesthetic value to humans. And the limitations or defects of any one species could be remedied genetically by reprograming.

Such dominion jeopardizes the life of all creation. Choosing to create new life forms constitutes an unprecedented invasion of the life-sustaining fabric of creation. The likely loss of genetic diversity—which is already occurring from the increased extinction of species because of human causes—would dwindle creation's ability to nurture future life . . .

The ability of genetic engineering to program mental and psychological functioning unleashes the power for molding a society to fit the norms of its rulers. Why not genetically eliminate social misfits? Why not genetically reinforce passive, conforming personality characteristics? Many regimes would find it tantalizing to reinforce their rule and quiet dissent through inward, genetic controls on its citizens rather than external force.

Such dangers may seem far-fetched, especially in pluralistic societies. But in capitalistic countries like the United States, genetic control first would be established not by the state, but by the marketplace. Every parent wants a perfect baby. If there are gene banks offering a variety of desired traits, people will pay to perfect their offspring.

Since wealth and power would determine who will have access to such choices, economic divisions would be genetically reinforced. Those with wealth would strive to improve their genetic riches. The end result would be a new basis for discrimination, inequality, and oppression, based no longer on race or class, but on genetic composition. A virtual biological caste system could potentially result.

From Auschwitz to Hiroshima to Love Canal, humanity has decisively demonstrated that its technological powers overwhelm its capacities for moral judgment. The genetic engineering of human life, if allowed to proceed, will quickly trespass any well-intentioned boundaries and guidelines. This technology is setting its own rules and tempting humanity with awesome powers. If grasped, such power will become intoxicating, and the pressure to seize all of it will be irresistible.

Humanity neither knows enough about the intricacies of life, nor possesses the moral discernment and spiritual wisdom to design "more perfect" human beings. Such actions claim prerogatives for humanity that rightly belong only to the Creator.

8 READING

A MARXIST VIEW OF THE GENETIC GENIE

The Guardian

The Guardian *defines itself as a radical independent newsweekly. It takes a Marxist point of view in its weekly coverage of national and international affairs.* The Guardian *is published by the Institute for Independent Social Journalism, a staff managed and operated cooperative. The Institute is a non-profit educational organization.* The Guardian *editors have expressed concern that serious social and moral dangers posed by genetic engineering will not be dealt with adequately.*

Points to Consider

1. How is the new science of genetic engineering described?
2. How is capitalism defined and what influence will it have on genetic engineering?
3. What specific dangers to society will arise from genetic research?
4. Why is a prohibition against research in genetic engineering proposed?

"DNA: Corporations Manipulate Life," *The Guardian,* September 17, 1980.

Under the present system—aggressive capitalism with the emphasis on profit for the few and exploitation for the many, militarism and racism—the ability to manipulate the genetic code is as dangerous as nuclear weapons.

A new era of scientific exploration has dawned, bringing with it some potential benefits for humankind but far, far greater dangers.

The average person knows nothing about this and is unable to exercise any control over a process which in a relatively short time could conceivably alter the course of human life and history.

Big business and its scientific associates know about it, of course, and are plunging headlong into a new profit venture, indifferent to possibly horrendous social consequences. The government is on the sidelines, cheering and spending $100 million a year paying for research.

The era began in the last decade with the development of recombinant DNA techniques, paving the way for genetic manipulation. It took a logical step forward this month with the announcement that Yale scientists had changed the genetic composition of two mice.

The state of the art may still be considered primitive, akin perhaps to the Wright brothers when they began to design the flights at Kitty Hawk. But in less time than it took the Wrights' successors to send a rocket to the moon, genetic technology may reach the point where it is possible to create not only advanced new life forms but to strategically manipulate the structure of human life itself.

DNA stands for deoxyribonucleic acid. It is the active material in the genes of all living things, constituting the genetic code which determines heredity. Recombinant DNA, gene-splicing, mixes and combines genes from animals, plants and viruses to produce new life forms and traits.

Inject Alien Genes

The Yale experiments on mice apparently proved it is possible to inject alien genes into newly fertilized mouse egg cells and have them become a permanent part of the embryo and living creature. The test showed that the genetic composition of an an-

56

imal can be changed. This process—changing heredity by introducing foreign genes—is known as genetic engineering.

Advances in this technology are taking place very rapidly, spurred forward by profit-hungry multinational corporations and a government which is not indifferent either to foreign competition or to the repressive potential of genetic research.

The biggest question now is when experiments are going to be made on human beings and whether the results in the long run will help or cripple the human race.

This question is not being answered by the forces which support increasing DNA research and development—big business, the government and most of the scientific community. Aside from a few voices of progressive scientists, all that's being talked about are potential gains in curing illnesses, correcting heredity defects, expanding food supply and the like. The ethical implications of the negative aspects, which are far greater, are either minimized or suppressed.

Proponents of genetic engineering never miss the opportunity to laugh off the catastrophic potential of DNA research.

Take scientist Norton Zinder of Rockefeller University, who replied to a query from Time magazine in these words: "No one's going to diddle with human embryos in a time frame we can understand. Maybe in a thousand years." Or listen to scientist Daniel Callahan of Hastings Center, quoted in Newsweek last week: "The idea of malevolent persons manufacturing human beings in a laboratory is still science fiction."

A Thousand Years?

We wonder whether these doctors would be willing to stake their own lives on such unscientific and simplistic predictions the way they are asking the human race to stake its life on them. The idea that scientists will be able to manipulate human genes in a few years but will not actually do so for a thousand years is pure duplicity, not pure science. And Callahan's comment equating a fear of what big corporations and the government will do with genetic research to a paranoid worry about Dr. Frankenstein is beneath contempt.

The heart of the matter isn't opposition to sophisticated scientific research. Such research and new technologies are inevitable and can be of tremendous service to humankind. The issue boils down to the political and social context within which this process unfolds—a context which may have benefited the top scientific community and its business and government cronies but which inspires the rest of thinking humanity with grave doubts to say the least.

Under the present system—aggressive capitalism with the

emphasis on profit for the few and exploitation for the many,
militarism and racism—the ability to manipulate the genetic
code is as dangerous as nuclear weapons.

What are some of these dangers? Presently, they include
threats to the health and safety of workers in the industries
which are producing new life forms; the possiblity of creating
new diseases; the chance of a biological "mistake" infecting
whole populations.

Nature of Danger

The nature of the danger will sharply increase in the next few
years as new breakthroughs take place. What new life forms will
private enterprise patent (having been given the right to do so
by the Supreme Court? What new advances in genetic manipulation will take place that will allow science to "correct" hereditary
problems in human embryos—leading to unknown consequences? (The question of "bad" genes is cropping up these
days in the chemical and other industries, with efforts being
made to screen out job applicants who are genetically "predis-
posed" to certain illnesses on the job rather than stressing the
elimination of workplace hazards and pollution by management.)

At what point will the government, business and scientific
community decide that certain genes—perhaps found in particular races—can be "improved" with a little manipulation? (This is
one of the biggest dangers of all, especially with eugenics theories making a comeback. The white racist argument that third
world people—and women—are genetically inferior has finally
acquired a technology which could change things.)

When will genetic research be applied to new biological
weapons systems? Is it impossible to conceive of a government
taking such research and seeking to create a new type of worker

58

or soldier? At what point, in essence, will the U.S. government decide it would be best for the capitalist system if human beings looked or thought or behaved differently than they do now?

One of the reasons these questions come to mind, aside from the nature of the social system which will acquire the benefits of DNA technology, is that the research and development into genetic techniques is virtually without regulation.

Washington has put forward some very limited guidelines for those establishments, usually universities, which are working with government money. But the research and production of private corporations—where much of the action is taking place—are governed only by the profit motive and a voluntary agreement to follow the federal guidelines with no serious enforcement provisions. The guidelines for funded research are weak and full of loopholes but the absence of any regulation of corporate endeavors is truly frightening.

Prohibition

As Marxists, we'd prefer a prohibition on genetic engineering under capitalism and restrictions under socialism. We think at minimum that the time is past due for genetic research in this country—particularly in the private sector—to at least be tightly regulated and controlled. Strict guidelines must be imposed swiftly. These should be designed not only by government bureaucrats and politicians in cooperation with big business but by representatives of the progressive scientific community and the public.

Under the political circumstances we also think there should be a campaign to prohibit any experimentation with altering human genes until all the safeguards required are put into operation.

Further, since DNA research is taking place in a number of countries and effects all humanity, we think an international body should be formed to set standards and oversee all scientific developments in this area, ultimately devising worldwide regulations. Even with government regulation, there would be nothing to stop a U.S. corporation from performing its research and production in a foreign country that did not have any regulations unless international controls existed.

Without question, recombinant DNA technology could be of some benefit to the people over the years. Under capitalism it could become a nightmare. Left and progressive forces should fight for whatever regulations and reforms are possible under the present system before it gets completely out of hand.

WHAT IS RELIGIOUS BIAS?

This activity may be used as an individualized study guide for students in libraries and resource centers or as a discussion catalyst in small group and classroom discussions.

Many readers are unaware that written material usually expresses an opinion or bias. The skill to read with insight and understanding requires the ability to detect different kinds of bias. Political bias, race bias, sex bias, ethnocentric bias and religious bias are five basic kinds of opinions expressed in editorials and literature that attempt to persuade. This activity will focus on religious bias defined in the glossary below.

FIVE KINDS OF EDITORIAL BIAS

*sex bias—the expression of dislike for and/or feeling of superiority over a person because of gender or sexual preference

*race bias—the expression of dislike for and/or feeling of superiority over a racial group

*ethnocentric bias—the expression of a belief that one's own group, race, religion, culture or nation is superior. Ethnocentric persons judge others by their own standards and values

*political bias—the expression of opinions and attitudes about government related issues on the local, state or international level

*religious bias—the expression of a religious belief or attitude.

Guidelines

Read through the following statements and decide which ones represent religious opinions or bias. Evaluate each statement by using the method indicated.

Place the letter (R) in front of any sentence that reflects religious opinion or bias.

Place the letter (N) in front of any sentence that does not reflect religious opinion or bias.

Place the letter (S) in front of any sentence that you are not sure about.

_____ 1. All religious leaders should oppose the development of biological weapons.

_____ 2. Human genetic engineering should be regulated by government agencies.

_____ 3. Religious traditions have left societies unprepared to deal with the moral dilemmas posed by genetic engineering.

_____ 4. In the future, parents may be able to choose from a library of genes in designing their own offspring.

_____ 5. With the possibility of human genetic engineering, human nature is no longer fixed. Science may be able to redesign human physical, mental and emotional traits.

_____ 6. Redesigning human traits violates God's plan for people on earth.

_____ 7. Genetic engineering is a technique with enormous potential for good and the nation should not adopt policies aimed at preventing development of this technology.

_____ 8. The profit motive and not public welfare will determine how human genetic engineering is used in the United States.

_____ 9. The U.S. Supreme Court has ruled that new forms of genetically engineered life could be granted patents.

_____10. Like nuclear physics, genetic engineering confers on human beings a power for which they are morally unprepared.

_____11. All science can and will be both used and abused.

_____12. Most religious traditions would endorse some human freedom to modify or transcend nature but would not endorse substantial changes in human physical and mental traits.

_____13. Genetic engineering offers brightened prospects for improving the lot of humanity.

_____14. The U.S. should not produce a genetically engineered biological weapon.

_____15. Biotechnology is providing the tools for designing human life according to predetermined specifications. Humans are about to acquire the power of authorship over human life itself.

Other Activities

1. Locate three examples of religious opinion or bias in the readings from chapters one or two.

2. Make up one statement that would be an example of each of the following: sex bias, race bias, ethnocentric bias, and political bias.

3. See if you can locate any factual statements in the fifteen items listed above.

C H A P T E R 3

ALTERING LIFE FOR PROFIT: IDEAS IN CONFLICT

PATENTING LIVING ORGANISMS

Office of Technology Assessment

The Office of Technology Assessment is an advisory board created by the United States Congress. Its purpose is to research and advise the Congress and general public about how new scientific and technological developments will influence the economic and social life of the nation. The advisory board is comprised of House and Senate members and members chosen from the research staffs of colleges and universities around the country.

Points to Consider:

1. What important ruling did the Supreme Court make regarding patent law?
2. How is the impact of this ruling described?
3. What do genetics and other biological sciences have in common?
4. Why has public concern increased over scientific research and developments?

Excerpted from *Impacts of Applied Genetics,* Office of Technology Assessment, Congress of the United States, 1981.

Continued advances in science and technology are beginning to provide choices that strain human value systems in areas where previously no choice was possible.

On June 16,1980, in a 5-to-4 decision, the Supreme Court ruled that a human-made micro-organism was patentable under Federal patent statutes. The decision, while hailed by some as assuring this country's technological future, was at the same time denounced by others as creating Aldous Huxleys "Brave New World". It will do neither.

The Patent Decision

1. Meaning and Scope of the Decision.—The decision held that a patent could not be denied on a genetically engineered micro-organism that otherwise met the legal requirements for patentability solely because it was alive. It was based on the Court's interpretation of a provision of the patent law which states that a patent may be granted on "... any new and useful ... manufacture, or composition of matter ..." (35 U.S.C. § 101).

It is uncertain whether the case will serve as a legal precedent for patenting more complex organisms. Such organisms, however, will probably not meet other legal prerequisites to patentability that were not at issue here. In any event, fears that the case would be legal precedent sometime in the distant future for patenting human beings are unfounded because the 13th amendment to the Constitution absolutely prohibits ownership of humans.

2. Impact on the Biotechnololgy Industry.—The decision is not crucial to the development of the industry. It will stimulate innovation by encouraging the dissemination of technical information that otherwise would have been maintained as trade secrets because patents are public documents that fully describe the inventions. In addition, the ability to patent genetically engineered micro-organisms will reduce the risks and uncertainties facing individual companies in the commercial development of those organisms and their products, but only to a limited degree because reasonably effective alternatives exist. These are: 1) maintaining the organisms as trade secrets; 2) patenting microbiological processes and their products; and 3) patenting inanimate components of micro-organisms, such as genetically engineered plasmids.

3. Impact on Academic Research.—Because the decision may encourage academic scientists to commercialize the results of

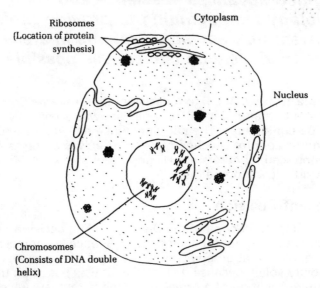

Cell Structure

Ribosomes (Location of protein synthesis)

Cytoplasm

Nucleus

Chromosomes (Consists of DNA double helix)

their research, it may inhibit the free exchange of information, but only if scientists rely on trade secrecy rather than patents to protect their inventions from competitors in the marketplace. In this respect, it is not clear how molecular biology differs from other research fields with commercial potential.

Genetics and Society

Continued advances in science and technology are beginning to provide choices that strain human value systems in areas where previously no choice was possible. Existing ethical and moral systems do not provide clear guidelines and directions for those choices. New programs, both in public institutions and in the popular media, have been established to explore the relationships among science, technology, society, and value systems, but more work needs to be done.

Genetics—and other areas of the biological sciences—have in common a much closer relationship to certain ethical questions than do most advances in the physical sciences or engineering. The increasing control over the characteristics of organisms and the potential for altering inheritance in a directed fashion raise again questions about the relationship of humans to each other and to other living things. People respond in different ways to this potential; some see it (like many predecessor developments in science) as a challenging opportunity, others as a threat, and still others respond with vague unease. Although many people cannot articulate fully the basis for their concern, ethical, moral, and religious reasons are often cited.

The public's increasing concern about the advance of science and impacts of technology has led to demands for greater participation in decisions concerned with scientific and technological issues, not only in the United States but throughout the world. The demands imply new challenges to systems of representative government. In every Western country, new mechanisms have been devised for increasing citizen participation.

The public has already become involved in decision-making with regard to genetics. As the science develops, additional issues in which the public will demand involvement can be anticipated for the years ahead. The question then becomes one of how best to involve the public in decision-making.

THE RIGHT TO PATENT LIFE: THE POINT

Chief Justice Warren Burger

A microbiologist, Ananda M. Chakrabarty, filed a patent relating to his invention of human-made, genetically engineered bacteria capable of breaking down multiple components of crude oil, a capability possessed by no naturally occurring bacteria. A patent examiner, Sidney A. Diamond, rejected the microbiologist's patent claim, ruling, among other things, that the bacteria, as living things, were not patentable subject matter under federal law (35 USCS Section 101). In Diamond v. Chakrabarty, 447 US 303, the United States Supreme Court reversed this decision. In an opinion by Chief Justice Burger, joined by Justices Stewart, Blackmun, Rehnquist, and Stevens, it was held that a live human-made micro-organism is patentable subject matter under federal law 35 USCS Section 101.

Points to Consider

1. What was the nature of the patent application by Chakrabarty?
2. How is the question before the court described?
3. What reasons are cited for granting the patent?
4. What does Chief Justice Burger say about environmental risks of genetic engineering?

Excerpted from Diamond v. Chakrabarty, 447 US 303 (1980).

Congress thus recognized that the relevant distinction was not between living and inanimate things, but between products of nature, whether living or not, and human-made inventions.

The question before us in this case is a narrow one of statutory interpretation requiring us to construe 35 USCS § 101, which provides:

"Whoever invents or discovers any new and useful process, machine, manufacture, or composition of matter, or any new and useful improvement thereof, may obtain a patent therefor, subject to the conditions and requirements of this title."

Specifically, we must determine whether respondent's micro-organism constitutes a "manufacture" or "composition of matter" within the meaning of the statute . . .

This Court has read the term "manufacture" in § 101 in accordance with its dictionary definition to mean "the production of articles for use from raw or prepared materials by giving to these materials new forms, qualities, properties, or combinations, whether by hand-labor or by machinery."

The History

The relevant legislative history also supports a broad construction. The Patent Act of 1793, authored by Thomas Jefferson, defined statutory subject matter as "any new and useful art, machine, manufacture, or composition of matter, or any new or useful improvement." The Act embodied Jefferson's philosophy that "ingenuity should receive a liberal encouragement . . ."

In 1952, when the patent laws were recodified, Congress replaced the word "art" with "process," but otherwise left Jefferson's language intact. The Committee Reports accompanying the 1952 Act inform us that Congress intended statutory subject matter to "include anything under the sun that is made by man."

This is not to suggest that section 101 has no limits or that it embraces every discovery. The laws of nature, physical phenomena, and abstract ideas have been held not patentable . . .

Thus, a new mineral discovered in the earth or a new plant found in the wild is not patentable subject matter. Likewise, Einstein could not patent his celebrated law that $E = mc^2$; nor could Newton have patented the law of gravity. Such discoveries are "manifestations of . . . nature, free to all men and reserved exclusively to none."

Judged in this light, respondent's micro-organism plainly

qualifies as patentable subject matter. His claim is not to a hitherto unknown natural phenomenon, but to a non-naturally occurring manufacture or composition of matter—a product of human ingenuity "having a distinctive name, character [and] use . . ."

Here, the patentee has produced a new bacterium with markedly different characteristics from any found in nature and one having the potential for significant utility. His discovery is not nature's handiwork, but his own; accordingly it is patentable subject matter under § 101.

Replication of DNA

When DNA replicates, the original strands unwind and serve as templates for the building of new complementary strands. The daughter molecules are exact copies of the parent, with each having one of the parent strands.

SOURCE: Office of Technology Assessment.

First Argument

Two contrary arguments are advanced, neither of which we find persuasive. The petitioner's first argument rests on the enactment of the 1930 Plant Patent Act, which afforded patent protection to certain asexually reproduced plants, and the 1970 Plant Variety Protection Act, which authorized protection for certain sexually reproduced plants but excluded bacteria from its protection. In the petitioner's view, the passage of these Acts evidences congressional understanding that the terms "manufacture" or "composition of matter" do not include living things; if they did, the petitioner argues, neither Act would have been necessary.

We reject this argument. Prior to 1930, two factors were thought to remove plants from patent protection. The first was the belief that plants, even those artificially bred, were products of nature for purposes of the patent law. This position appears to have derived from the decision of the Patent Office in Latimer, 1889, in which a patent claim for fiber found in the needle of the Pinus australis was rejected. The Commissioner reasoned that a contrary result would permit "patents [to] be obtained upon the trees of the forest and the plants of the earth, which of course would be unreasonable and impossible." The Latimer case, it seems, came to "set forth the general stand taken in these matters" that plants were natural products not subject to patent protection.

The second obstacle to patent protection for plants was the fact that plants were thought not amenable to the "written description" requirement of the patent law. Because new plants may differ from old only in color or perfume, differentiation by written description was often impossible.

In enacting the Plant Patent Act, Congress addressed both of these concerns. It explained at length its belief that the work of the plant breeder "in aid of nature" was patentable invention. No Committee or Member of Congress, however, expressed the broader view, now urged by the petitioner, that the terms "manufacture" or "composition of matter" exclude living things. The sole support for that position in the legislative history of the 1930 Act is found in the conclusory statement of Secretary of Agriculture Hyde, in a letter to the Chairmen of the House and Senate Committees considering the 1930 Act, that "the patent laws ... at the present time are understood to cover only inventions or discoveries in the field of inanimate nature." Secretary Hyde's opinion, however, is not entitled to controlling weight. His views were solicited on the administration of the new law and not on the scope of patentable subject matter—an area beyond his competence. Moreover, there is language in the House and Senate Committee Reports suggesting that to the extent Congress considered the matter it found the Secretary's dichotomy unpersuasive. The reports observe:

"There is a clear and logical distinction between the discovery of a new variety of plant and of certain inanimate things, such, for example, as a new and useful natural mineral. The mineral is created wholly by nature unassisted by man. . . . On the other hand, a plant discovery resulting from cultivation is unique, isolated, and is not repeated by nature, nor can it be reproduced by nature unaided by man. . . ."

Congress thus recognized that the relevant distinction was not between living and inanimate things, but between products of nature, whether living or not, and human-made inventions. Here, respondent's micro-organism is the result of human ingenuity and research . . .

Second Argument

The petitioner's second argument is that micro-organisms cannot qualify as patentable subject matter until Congress expressly authorizes such protection. Its position rests on the fact that genetic technology was unforeseen when Congress enacted section 101. From this it is argued that resolution of the patentability of inventions such as respondent's should be left to Congress. The legislative process, the petitioner argues, is best equipped to weigh the competing economic, social, and scientific considerations involved, and to determine whether living organisms produced by genetic engineering should receive patent protection . . .

It is, of course, correct that Congress, not the courts, must define the limits of patentability; but it is equally true that once Congress has spoken it is "the province and duty of the judicial department to say what the law is."

Congress has performed its constitutional role in defining patentable subject matter in section 101; we perform ours in construing the language Congress has employed . . .

Grave Risks

To buttress its argument, the petitioner points to grave risks that may be generated by research endeavors such as respondent's. The briefs present a gruesome parade of horribles. Scientists, among them Nobel laureates, are quoted suggesting that genetic research may pose a serious threat to the human race, or, at the very least, that the dangers are far too substantial to permit such research to proceed apace at this time. We are told that genetic research and related technological developments may spread pollution and disease, that it may result in a loss of genetic diversity, and that its practice may tend to depreciate the value of human life. These arguments are forcefully, even passionately presented; they remind us that, at times, human ingenuity seems unable to control fully the forces it creates—that, with Hamlet, it is sometimes better "to bear those ills we have than fly to others that we know not of."

It is argued that this Court should weigh these potential hazards in considering whether respondent's invention is patentable subject matter. We disagree. The grant or denial of patents on micro-organisms is not likely to put an end to genetic research or to its attendant risks. The large amount of research that has already occurred when no researcher had sure knowledge that patent protection would be available suggests that legislative or judicial fiat as to patentability will not deter the scientific mind from probing into the unknown any more than Canute could command the tides. Whether respondent's claims are patentable may determine whether research efforts are accelerated by the hope of reward or slowed by want of incentives, but that is all.

What is more important is that we are without competence to entertain these arguments—either to brush them aside as fantasies generated by fear of the unknown, or to act on them. The choice we are urged to make is a matter of high policy for resolution within the legislative process after the kind of investigation, examination, and study that legislative bodies can provide and courts cannot. That process involves the balancing of competing values and interests, which in our democratic system is the business of elected representatives. Whatever their validity, the contentions now pressed on us should be addressed to the political branches of the Government, the Congress and the Executive, and not the courts.

THE RIGHT TO PATENT LIFE: THE COUNTERPOINT

Justice William J. Brennan, Jr.

In the case Diamond v. Chakrabarty, Justice William Brennan dissented from the majority. Joined by Justices White, Marshall and Powell, he expressed the view that Congress had indicated its belief through prior statutes regulating the patenting of plants that living organisms are not patentable.

Points to Consider

1. What is the purpose of patent laws?
2. How has Congress, through its laws, addressed the issue of patenting living or animate inventions?
3. What was the Plant Patent Act of 1930?
4. Why does Justice Brennan believe that living organisms should not be patentable?

Excerpted from Diamond v. Chakrabarty, 447 US 303 (1980).

Congress has included bacteria within the focus of its legislative concern, but not within the scope of patent protection.

I agree with the Court that the question before us is a narrow one. Neither the future of scientific research, nor even the ability of respondent Chakrabarty to reap some monopoly profits from his pioneering work, is at stake. Patents on the processes by which he has produced and employed the new living organism are not contested. The only question we need decide is whether Congress, exercising its authority under Article I Section 8, of the Constitution, intended that he be able to secure a monopoly on the living organism itself, no matter how produced or how used. Because I believe the Court has misread the applicable legislation, I dissent.

The patent laws attempt to reconcile this Nation's deep-seated antipathy to monopolies with the need to encourage progress . . .

Given the complexity and legislative nature of this delicate task, we must be careful to extend patent protection no further than Congress has provided. In particular, were there an absence of legislative direction, the courts should leave to Congress the decisions whether and how far to extend the patent privilege into areas where the common understanding has been that patents are not available.

In this case, we do not confront a complete legislative vacuum. The sweeping language of the Patent Act of 1793, as re-enacted in 1952, is not the last pronouncement Congress has made in this area. In 1930 Congress enacted the Plant Patent Act affording patent protection to developers of certain asexually reproduced plants. In 1970 Congress enacted the Plant Variety Protection Act to extend protection to certain new plant varieties capable of sexual reproduction. Thus, we are not dealing—as the Court would have it—with the routine problem of "unanticipated inventions."

In these two Acts Congress has addressed the general problem of patenting animate inventions and has chosen carefully limited language granting protection to some kinds of discoveries, but specifically excluding others. These Acts strongly evidence a congressional limitation that excludes bacteria from patentability.

Living Organisms

First, the Acts evidence Congress' understanding, at least since 1930, that Section 101 does not include living organisms. If

75

newly developed living organisms not naturally occurring had been patentable under Section 101, the plants included in the scope of the 1930 and 1970 Acts could have been patented without new legislation. Those plants, like the bacteria involved in this case, were new varieties not naturally occurring . . .

I cannot share the Court's implicit assumption that Congress was engaged in either idle exercises or mere correction of the public record when it enacted the 1930 and 1970 Acts. And Congress certainly thought it was doing something significant. The Committee Reports contain expansive prose about the previously unavailable benefits to be derived from extending patent protection to plants.

Because Congress thought it had to legislate in order to make agricultural "human-made inventions" patentable and because the legislation Congress enacted is limited, it follows that Con-

The Replication of DNA

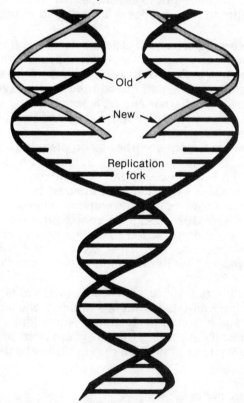

When DNA replicates, the original strands unwind and serve as templates for the building of new complementary strands.

Uncorking The Bottle

The People's Business Commission, a non-profit educational foundation that filed a brief against the patent certification, said the Court's ruling, combined with the lack of any regulation of industrial genetic engineering research and development, has "(let the genie) out of the bottle before most Americans have even realized that the bottle was uncorked."

Guardian Editorial, June, 1980

gress never meant to make items outside the scope of the legislation patentable.

Second, the 1970 Act clearly indicates that Congress has included bacteria within the focus of its legislative concern, but not within the scope of patent protection. Congress specifically excluded bacteria from the coverage of the 1970 Act. The Court's attempts to supply explanations for this explicit exclusion ring hollow. It is true that there is no mention in the legislative history of the exclusion, but that does not give us license to invent reasons. The fact is that Congress, assuming that animate objects as to which it had not specifically legislated could not be patented, excluded bacteria from the set of patentable organisms.

The Court's Decision

As I have shown, the Court's decision does not follow the unavoidable implications of the statute. Rather, it extends the patent system to cover living material even though Congress plainly has legislated in the belief that Section 101 does not encompass living organisms. It is the role of Congress, not this Court, to broaden or narrow the reach of the patent laws. This is especially true where, as here, the composition sought to be patented uniquely implicates matters of public concern.

12

IDEAS IN CONFLICT

COMMERCIALIZING LIFE: A SOCIALIST VIEW

The People

The People *is the official publication of the Socialist Labor Party headquartered in Palo Alto, California. The following statement sets forth the Socialist Labor Party's view toward the possibilities and dangers of revolutionary new gene splicing technology. Fears about the profit motive controlling this new scientific research are expressed.*

Points to Consider

1. What are the dangers of corporate control?
2. Why are safeguards inadequate for research in genetic engineering?
3. How will profit motives influence the new science of genetic research?
4. What should be done to prevent the social dangers presented by the genetic engineering industry?

"Genetic Engineering," *The People,* November 15, 1980.

The profit motive will lead to research done in reckless disregard of safety for the sake of the quick development of new genetic commodities.

"Science + Capitalism = Danger."

The truth of this equation is confirmed by recent developments in genetic engineering, in which deoxyribonucleic acid (DNA), the basic determinant of heredity, is altered by the insertion of new genes. On October 14, Wall Street was hit by a frenzy of trading in a newly offered genetic-engineering stock. One million shares of Genentech, a pioneer firm in the field, went on sale on the open market. The initial $35-a-share price was rapidly pushed up to $89. The Wall Street Journal described it as "the most striking price explosion on a new stock within the memory of most stockbrokers. . . ."

The orgy of speculative buying and selling reflected the hopes that genetic engineering will prove a lucrative source of new profits. Genetically altered bacteria, for example, can be used to provide a wide range of biological commodities having potential profitable uses in medicine, pharmacology and other fields.

Genentech is in the forefront of the genetic-engineering industry. The four-year-old company has already used gene-splicing technology to manufacture human insulin, growth hormone and interferon, an antiviral substance that may prove useful in fighting cancer.

Genentech is also in the forefront of the controversy surrounding genetic engineering. It has already paid the University of California-San Francisco $350,000 to settle a claim that the company improperly used the work of university researchers in its synthesis of human growth hormone. Genentech's joint venture with the pharmaceutical firm Hoffmann-La Roche in cloning interferon genes has lead to a second lawsuit involving charges of stealing the work of other researchers.

Dangers of Corporate Control

The lawsuits and a U.S. Supreme Court decision that newly created organisms can be patented point to one of the dangers of mixing profit-making and scientific research—the possibility that basic scientific knowledge will be expropriated and locked up behind the veil of corporate trade secrets.

Harvard University is already considering a plan to set up a genetic-engineering firm for the commercial exploitation of its gene-splicing discoveries. Several other universities, including

Emergence of New Biotechnology Firms, 1977-83

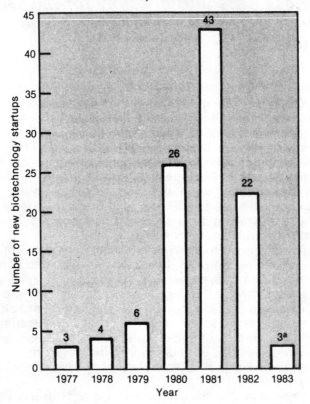

[a]As of November 1983.

SOURCE: Office of Technology Assessment.

Stanford, Yale, Massachusetts Institute of Technology and the University of California, may follow suit.

The potential benefits of gene splicing will become available for use only when private profit interests so dictate. Moreover, the profit motive will lead to research done in reckless disregard of safety for the sake of the quick development of new genetic commodities.

The dangers involved in profit-motivated genetic engineering are frightening. New combinations of genes have unpredictable effects. As Harvard biologist George Wald has pointed out, "Single genes do not operate independently of one another. Scientists are in no position to predict what implanted foreign genes can or will do." Thus, according to Wald, "Going ahead in this direction may not only be unwise, but dangerous. Potentially it could breed new animal and plant diseases, new sources of cancer, novel epidemics."

In addition to the dangers posed to the health and safety of genetic-engineering workers, there is the danger that genetically altered organisms could escape from laboratories to plague the population at large. This danger is magnified by genetic engineering carried out on the commercial scale. Safeguards that can be imposed on small research laboratories will undoubtedly be considered too costly to be imposed on mass commercial operations.

Inadequate 'Safeguards'

The National Institutes of Health (NIH) nominally bear the responsibility for "safeguards" on genetic research. In the 1970s, an outpouring of criticism by leading biologists led to a temporary voluntary moratorium on genetic engineering research and to the development by the NIH of guidelines for laboratory safety for government-funded research. In an effort to head off mandatory regulation, industry and independently funded researchers promised to abide by the NIH guidelines.

Unfortunately, the guidelines are weak. For example, in developing them, the NIH's "worst-case" experiment used the weakest strain of bacteria then available. There have also been a number of breaches of the guidelines. In perhaps the most notorious case to date, Samuel Kennedy, a researcher at the medical school of the University of California at San Diego, cloned the wrong virus—one which it was not permissible to clone under the guidelines then in effect.

Brave New World

Concerns about Brave New World applications of genetic engineering have been raised and usually dismissed as impossible. But already, recombinant cells have been introduced and found to function in living animals.

As David Suzuki, a geneticist, wrote three years ago, "What could be more explosive than the application in human engineering of techniques of molecular genetics . . . in a society in which racism, bigotry, greed, and economic inequities are apparent?"

Katherine Yih, *Guardian*, 1980

In other cases, scientists apparently violated the guidelines deliberately in order to beat out their competitors. What may have happened in privately funded research is not known because there are no enforcement mechanisms to ensure compliance with the guidelines. Despite these violations, the NIH has loosened the guidelines twice within the past year. It is hardly accidental that the guidelines have been relaxed at the very time profit-making applications of genetic engineering are on the rise.

As for controlling commercial research, the NIH's actions are akin to locking the barn door after the horse has been stolen. Though corporate spending has already reached the multimillion-dollar-a-year level and products are already being marketed, an NIH advisory committee voted September 26 to do no more than establish a subcommittee to look into possible regulation of large-scale gene splicing.

Antisocial Ends

Accidents aren't the only dangers posed by genetic engineering. Even more frightening are the deliberately antisocial ends toward which capitalism is likely to direct genetic engineering. The same class that has used scientific knowledge to create nuclear bombs and nerve gases can hardly be trusted to use genetic engineering in a socially responsible manner. Gene-splicing technology could easily open the door to new biological weapons of unprecedented barbarity. Nor can attempts to manipulate human heredity to produce "improved" human beings be ruled out.

Preventing the use of genetic engineering for such antisocial ends and ensuring that its potentially useful applications and products are developed safely require freeing scientific research from the distorting and dangerous control of the profit motive. (Scientific knowledge can be made to serve useful social ends only when it is placed under the rational democratic control of a socialist society.)

GENETIC ENGINEERING: A BUSINESS PERSPECTIVE

John P. Abbott

John Abbott presents Shell Oil Company's outlook on the future of genetic engineering. Writing in Shell News, *he describes the plans and visions that the Shell Oil Company has for the science of biotechnology. Biotechnology is the term used for the industrial and business applications of research in genetic engineering.*

Points to Consider

1. Why is an oil company interested in the new gene splicing technology?
2. What is the meaning of the term "recombinant DNA technology?"
3. What will the future of this technology mean for business?
4. Why is Shell Oil Company interested in interferon?

John Abbott, "Biotechnology," *Shell News,* volume 52, number 1, 1984, pp. 13–17.

"DNA recombination in biology is similar to the advent of the silicon chip in the computer industry."

What's an oil company doing trying to help in the treatment of cancer?

Dick Love has heard the question before. Soft-spoken and articulate, the former head of Shell's Biological Business Development is now president of Triton Biosciences Inc., a wholly owned Shell subsidiary conducting research on health products, including interferon, a possible cancer fighter.

"One of the milestones we've set for ourselves in this venture is to actually produce a product—an interferon—that will help in the treatment of cancer," he admits. "Another objective, one I think we've accomplished, was simply to gain an understanding of the biotechnology field and determine if it would be good for Shell's existing businesses in some manner. The first applications of the new technology will be in pharmaceuticals, but that

Breakdown of Japan's Expenditures for Recombinant DNA Technology R&D, Fiscal Year 1981

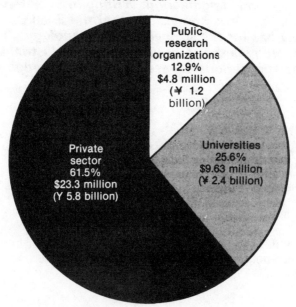

Public research organizations
12.9%
$4.8 million
(¥ 1.2 billion)

Universities
25.6%
$9.63 million
(¥ 2.4 billion)

Private sector
61.5%
$23.3 million
(Y 5.8 billion)

Total rDNA expenditure = $38.1 million (¥ 9.5 billion)

SOURCE: Office of Technology Assessment, based on data from *Science and Technology in Japan*, April/June 1983.

may be just the tip of the iceberg. Eventually, we may be able to translate that technology into other fields, including the chemical and petroleum business."

Translating the gains in biology to business isn't as farfetched as we might think. "The same basic technology of working with genes in human cells applies to working with genes in plant cells," Love points out. "In agriculture, for instance, we've always treated plants with herbicides and insecticides to help the farmer maximize his yield. Now we can approach the problem from a different angle—by working on the genetics of plants. Eventually we might end up with seeds that have characteristics to ward off insects, that grow quicker, that grow healthier."

A recent series of scientific break-throughs, based on the development of recombinant DNA technology—gene splicing to the layman—has changed the profile of classical biology. What had been scarcely imaginable by biologists in the past—the turn-of-the-century aviator's flight to the moon—now is suddenly, tantalizingly, within reach. "DNA recombination in biology is similar to the advent of the silicon chip in the computer industry," says Jeff Collins, Triton's director of Therapeutics. "The interferon project allows us to become familiar with recombinant DNA technology. Once we thoroughly understand it, we may be able to apply it in other Shell business . . ."

Interferon

"In a human, there are about one million pages of information—genes—scattered among 46 volumes—chromosomes," says Leo Kim, research associate in Shell's Agriculture Biotechnology Department. "Biotechnology allows you to turn to the right volume and the right page and cut out precisely the right word you're looking for. You can snip out that particular message and insert it into another organism that will produce a given product according to the directions of the new gene."

One area that is likely to be affected by the scientific break-throughs spurred by the development of biotechnology is interferon research. Until 1981, interferons—natural proteins manufactured by the body that "interfere" with virus diseases and cancer—were produced primarily from human white blood cells. The process was time-consuming, and because of short supply, the costs were staggering, as much as $30,000 per patient in some cases. The technology simply didn't exist to synthetically produce large quantities of pure interferon at relatively cheap cost. It soon became apparent, however, that recombinant DNA technology might solve these problems. "We recognized that there was going to be a major change in the way medicine would be practiced in the future, and that's what we think gives us the opportunity to enter the field," Love points out . . . 85

Health Care

"Health care is a huge industry in the United States, accounting for nearly one-tenth of our gross national product. The profit margins are attractive, particularly in the pharmaceutical companies, because the products generally are patented, and therefore, protected. It's also a highly technological business. That appealed to us because technology is one of our strengths. But the real opportunity came when we realized what was happening in the field of advanced biology and genetic engineering," he notes.

Most of the research activity so far has occurred in university medical hospitals. "They not only have a strong fundamental research effort in-house, but they also have the patient population necessary for the extensive testing required by the FDA," Love says. The first phase of clinical trials of Triton's Beta interferon were concluded recently at Stanford University, the University of Wisconsin, and the Common Cold Unit in England, world renowned for its testing of various agents against cold viruses. The Triton/Cetus venture is currently the only project in the country working on a Beta interferon produced by genetic engineering technology . . .

"During the inital stages, we tested 23 people who had cancer and had been unresponsive to other available treatments. Some are continuing to receive the interferon. At this stage of the trials we were trying to find out how much of the compound can be tolerated in the individual," Love says. "So far we've learned that our interferon is very well tolerated, better tolerated than most others, in fact. But we don't have any conclusion about whether or not this helped the patients at all.

"We'll soon go into a number of other clinical trials where we'll start getting answers to questions about its effectiveness against various types of cancer and virus diseases. The whole process will take about three years to complete, but a lot of difficult research still has to be done on the clinical applications of interferon, not to mention securing FDA approval of interferon.

We still have a number of hurdles to get across," he notes, "but if everything goes well, and interferon is effective in chemotherapy, we hope to be marketing it by 1987."

Interferon has shown activity against a number of diseases besides cancer, including shingles, rabies, hepatitis B, chickenpox, multiple sclerosis and even the common cold. It has stopped the growth of microbes causing diseases such as Rocky Mountain spotted fever and malaria, and helped reduce the chance of infections in patients with kidney transplants. "Most of the activity demonstrated so far has been in the laboratory." Love cautions, "Extensive human testing is just beginning."

Cancer Research

Love points out that the advances in molecular biology lend themselves especially well to diseases like cancer. "We are actually looking at how cells grow and what causes the cell to change; in the case of cancer, what causes it to go aberrant, rather than to do what it's supposed to do. In the past, cancer therapy was de-emphasized in many pharmaceutical companies' research programs because the technology didn't exist to study it adequately, and many products had very bad side effects. That explains why cancer research is not overcrowded in a business sense." He also points to a recent survey conducted by the company that queried 50 of the country's top scientists about important medical breakthroughs to come in the next decade. They listed cancer as the area most likely to experience the greatest changes in diagnosis and therapy.

"We hope what we learn from our cancer research will be applicable to other areas, like cardiovascular diseases for instance, maybe even central nervous system disorders," John Cole, Triton's director of Research, says. "In fact, a vast number of diseases may be linked to defective genes. For one reason or another, the genetic code that characterizes a cell gets scrambled. The system breaks down. We want to know why."

The Future

"Shell isn't trying to change its image," Love emphasizes. "But most people recognize that if we want to keep growing we're going to have to look beyond our traditional businesses. We know that the petrochemical business doesn't have the growth prospects it had 20 years ago. Naturally that doesn't mean we should abandon areas where our strengths lie. Instead, we should take advantage of what we do best—our technology, our organizational expertise, our many skills—and seize the opportunity when we have the chance. That's what gave birth to this idea of emerging businesses.

OPEN FORUM

This activity may be used as an individualized study guide for students in libraries and resource centers or as a discussion catalyst in small group and classroom discussions.

Guidelines

Democratic societies are usually open forums for opinions from all kinds of sources and groups. The press in democratic nations usually reflects the diversity and complexity of attitudes and ideas that surround social issues and conflicts. Examine the statements below that present different interpretations. Then evaluate the statements as indicated.

Mark (A) for any statement that you agree with.
Mark (B) for any statement that you disagree with.
Mark (N) for any statement that you are uncertain about.

_____ 1. The desire to be like God is becoming a technological possibility through human genetic engineering.

_____ 2. Ownership is the central religious and moral issue and the Bible declares that creation is God's and not ours to exploit economically as we see fit.

_____ 3. Patenting living organisms is an absurd concept and should not be permitted.

_____ 4. It is foolish to do everything that technology allows us to do.

_____ 5. The hope of economic returns for genetic engineering discount the future threats and risks of the technology.

_____ 6. The ability of genetic engineering to program mental and psychological functioning unleashes the power for molding a society to fit the norms of its leaders.

_____ 7. People who know that they are at risk for having a child with a genetic disease should not have children unless they are willing to pay for all the medical expenses.

_____ 8. No one has the right to bear children if they will suffer.

_____ 9. No one has the right to bear children if they will be a burden to society.

_____10. People should be allowed to choose the sex of their children by any means available.

_____11. In vitro fertilization and artificial insemination by donor are unnatural and should not be allowed.

_____12. A genetic screening test should be a requirement before couples can get a marriage license.

_____13. Hemophilia carriers should not have children of their own.
_____14. Pregnant women over age 38 should always have amniocentesis.
_____15. Society has no right to interfere with scientific freedom in genetic research.

CHAPTER 4

ENVIRONMENTAL EFFECTS OF GENETIC ENGINEERING

READINGS

BIOTECHNOLOGY AND THE ENVIRONMENT

Albert Gore, Jr.

Albert Gore, Jr. is a democratic congressman from Tennessee. He has been a congressional leader in examining the role of Congress in the oversight and regulation of research in genetic engineering.

Points to Consider

1. How did the gypsy moth arrive in the United States?
2. What is the lesson of the gypsy moth?
3. Why are the organisms being created today potentially so dangerous to the environment?

Testimony by Albert Gore, Jr., before the House Subcommittee on Science, Research and Technology, 1983.

The organisms that are being created today through genetic engineering are far more exotic than any creatures that have existed before. These are organisms with completely new genotypes, and, consequently, their potential for environmental damage could be far greater than for any "natural" organism.

In the late 1860's, a French astronomer named Leopold Trouvelot brought into this country a few eggs of a relatively obscure variety of European moth. Living at the time in Medford, Mass., Trouvelot kept these eggs and the moths that hatched from them at his home, as he tried in vain to breed a new, disease-resistant form of silk worm. As luck would have it, a few of Trouvelot's prized creatures escaped.

From this insignificant beginning, the gypsy moth ranks today as one of the most disastrous environmental pests in this Nation's history. In 1981 alone, gypsy moths defoliated over 10 million acres of trees around the country.

The tale of the gypsy moth is instructive, for it provides many lessons about the potential that exists for large-scale environmental damage from very small beginnings. It is not an isolated example. Like dutch elm disease, chestnut blight, and countless other examples, including kudzu in my native Tennessee—and if there are any southerners in the audience, you know what kudzu is—like all of these examples, the gypsy moth illustrates the problems that can occur when new foreign organisms are introduced into our environment.

In the mid-1970's, as recombinant DNA technology became widely utilized in laboratory experiments, great public concern arose over the possibility that some deadly new virus, or chemical kudzu, might escape from a lab and endanger surrounding populations. In response to this concern, guidelines for experiments were developed, and today genetic engineering experiments are carried out with relative safety in the labs. Indeed, we can all share the luxury of assuming that those early concerns were overblown.

The Environment

As concern over threats to public health have subsided, however, a new set of concerns about genetic engineering has developed. These concerns entail not human health, but the safety

92

of the environment. They emanate out of a fear not so much that an organism will escape, but that its deliberate release will produce serious ecological consequences.

Over the last several years, the commercial applications of biotechnology in both industry and agriculture have blossomed tremendously. In agriculture, new varieties of genetically engineered plants are being created, and new genetically engineered pesticides are being manufactured. In industry, microbes are

Gene Splicing Could Find Vaccine For Malaria

The malaria infection begins when a person is bitten by an *Anopheles* mosquito that bears *Plasmodia*. Sporozoites (1) are injected into the bloodstream, where they may remain for only 30 minutes before they infect liver cells. Within the liver cells, each sporozoite divides into six to twenty-four merozoites, the next *Palsmodium* life-stage. Merozoites burst from the infected liver cell (2) destroying it, and enter the blood stream, where they infect red blood cells and proliferate. In subsequent waves of infection, merozoites burst from the red blood cells and spread to other red blood cells. Red blood cells infected with merozoites may produce new cell surface molecules which allow them to bind to blood vessel walls (3). Some of the merozoites go on to become gametophytes, the next life-stage (4). These gametophytes are picked up by another *Anopheles* mosquito in another bite; they reproduce within the mosquito and form sporozoites, which may be injected into another person to begin the cycle anew.

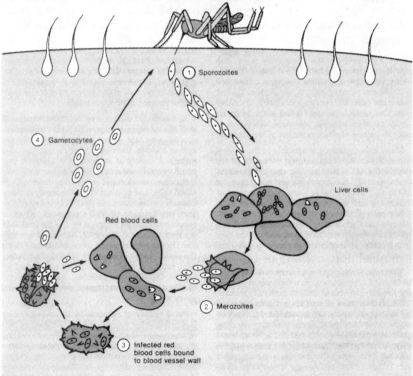

being developed to break down toxic waste, clean up oil spills, produce new forms of energy, and perform countless other tasks. We have even seen the creation of "super mice," announced last December, in experiments aimed at improving animal husbandry.

One of my constituents asked me why we wanted to make mice twice as large as normal mice and speculated as to whether the surplus cheese problem might have something to do with that.

All of these developments unquestionably have great potential benefits for our society. But the commercial success of these applications of biotechnology will ultimately depend upon their ability to be introduced into the environment on a widespread basis.

Already steps are being taken to introduce new organisms into the environment. The National Institutes of Health Recombinant DNA Advisory Committee has approved field tests for three new genetically engineered plants, and undoubtedly many more requests for field tests will soon be forthcoming.

Soon there will be efforts to conduct field tests of microbes as well. It is the increasing likelihood of such deliberate releases on a broader scale—as biotechnology moves out of the laboratory and into the environment—that causes concern over environmental impacts.

The organisms that are being created today through genetic engineering are far more exotic than any creatures that have existed before. These are organisms with completely new genotypes, and, consequently, their potential for environmental damage could be far greater than for any "natural" organism. It is important, therefore, that we understand all the potential environmental ramifications of an organism before it is released into an ecosystem—instead of waiting and finding out about them after the damage has occurred.

At the same time, however, as we consider the issues raised by the introduction of these organisms into the environment, we have to be careful not to unduly inhibit their development. Our society has much to gain from these uses of biotechnology. It is simply the case that we can benefit even more from the commercial applications of biotechnology if we utilize them in an environmentally safe manner.

We must examine the environmental implications of the new technology and the question of environmental impacts. We must examine the potential benefits to be reaped from the technology and consider how we should balance these benefits against any environmental risks that may exist. And we must consider what role the Federal Government should play in all of this.

ENVIRONMENTAL RISKS OF GENETIC ENGINEERING

Martin Alexander

Dr. Martin Alexander is a professor in the Department of Agronomy at Cornell University, Ithaca, New York. In the following statement he describes the many potential risks and environmental dangers of research in genetic engineering. He advocates a regulatory procedure to guard against potential environmental hazards.

Points to Consider

1. What does history say about the environmental risks of introducing new technologies?
2. What are the five components of risk?
3. Why do containment facilities in research laboratories sometimes fail?
4. Why can genetic changes made by humans spread in the environment?
5. What is the prudent course of action?

Excerpted from testimony by Martin Alexander before the House Subcommittee on Science, Research and Technology, 1983.

It is possible to distinguish five components of risk associated with the release of organisms with new and novel genotypes. Each component has a probability of occurring ranging from zero to one hundred percent.

At the outset, I should state my belief that genetic engineering will greatly benefit mankind. I feel that we are at the start of a period when major changes will occur in agriculture, industry, and technologies to maintain environmental quality as a result of the creation of new and novel genotypes. In agriculture, new varieties of plants will be introduced, and we shall see vaccines and other products to enhance beef and milk production. Industries concerned with chemical manufacturing, pharmaceuticals and food products will also benefit greatly from these developments. I am also convinced that we shall see new organisms and biotechnologies to destroy pollutants that are otherwise only slowly destroyed by biological mechanisms.

Risk of New Technology

On the other hand, the history of the introduction of technologies has much to teach us. In many instances, the risks of these technologies were not initially evident, but they became quite clear as the technology became widespread. Often, the risk occurred at a very low frequency, but the impact was quite large. Radiation therapy was a boon to medicine early in this century, but its use resulted in radiation sickness. Antibiotics revolutionized our approach to chemotherapy, but a not insignificant number of people suffered severe and often irreversible conseqences from the use of the wonder drugs. DDT prevented an enormous amount of human misery and widespread mortality resulting from insect vectors of human, animal and crop diseases, but the harmful effect of this insecticide became evident with time. The industrial revolution improved our standard of living and provided materials which would never have been available otherwise, but it was the prelude to air pollution. Atomic energy offers enormous promise where fuels for energy production are in short supply, but many people feel that the dangers are quite substantial. The proponents of these technologies, and many others that could be cited, minimized or ignored the risks in the past or still do so. The lure of major benefits from these new technologies has been so great that their proponents have been

96

unwilling to consider the possible undesirable consequences. Few, if any, major technologies have been introduced without some untoward effect.

With regard to the possible ecological consequences arising from the inadvertent or deliberate release of new genetic materials into waters and soils, I for one do not know whether there will or will not be an undesirable effect, but I believe we can assess the probability of a detrimental influence on humans, other species or the function of natural environments.

It is possible to distinguish five components of risk associated with the release of organisms with new and novel genotypes. Each component has a probability of occurring ranging from zero to one hundred percent. These risk components are: (1) the chance of release into a natural environment, (2) the possibility that the organism will survive there, (3) the likelihood that it will grow in that environment, (4) the possibility that it will make contact with species that it can injure, and (5) the chance that it will be harmful. If the new life form is deliberately released to perform some useful environmental function, and it does what is expected of it, only the last two factors need to be considered; that is, will it make contact with a species that it can harm and will it bring about that deleterious change . . .

'OK, I give up, Hopkins . . . What's green and red and eats lab technicians?'

Containment Facilities

Some individuals argue that the containment facilities in laboratories working with new genotypes will prevent the inadvertent discharge of any harmful organism. In this country and abroad, there are facilities which have excellent containment, and these laboratories are staffed with individuals who have spent years in acquiring skills to prevent release of the harmful organisms with which they work. However, even with these highly trained individuals and with presumably excellent containment facilities, inadvertent releases of disease-producing organisms have occurred. In this country, for example, at both the Center for Disease Control and the Plum Island facility, where work is done with highly contagious organisms, occasional accidents and consequent discharges have taken place. If these releases have taken place in the best of our facilities and with highly trained individuals, one can only speculate what might occur with individuals who are not well trained in containing potentially hazardous organisms, with individuals who do not take the issues seriously, with no monitoring or effective regulation of their actions, and with facilities that are far from the best.

It is also argued that organisms introduced into environments in which they are not indigenous will not survive. This view is completely contrary to an enormous body of scientific information. Although most species that are introduced into alien environments do in fact die out, the scientific literature contains numerous examples, some of which come from our studies, showing that many microorganisms are able to survive days, weeks, months, and even years although these species were not present in the environment before their deliberate introduction.

It is also argued that an introduced organism will not grow in an environment in which it is not native. This too is contrary to the existing body of scientific information. Admittedly, few species multiply in environments in which they were initially alien. However, examples are easily found of species that have proliferated even though they were not present in that habitat before. For example, farmers in the midwest and elsewhere regularly introduce a microorganism into soil that causes nitrogen fixation after it infects soybean roots. This microorganism was not previously present in many of these soils, but after it was deliberately introduced, it was able to survive and it did indeed proliferate. Moreover, it has a major effect on plant growth, but fortunately in this instance, the effect is highly beneficial.

Let me emphasize that a small percentage of the individual microorganisms in the enormous populations worked with in the laboratory and in industry will likely escape. Most of the species that are released into waters and soils will not survive, but a few will. Most of those species which survive in natural environments will probably not multiply; however, some will. Thus, the probability associated with each of these risk factors cannot be deemed to be zero. It may be very small, but it is not zero.

Furthermore, differing from chemicals, air pollutants, and radiation, microorganisms are able to increase in abundance. The problem of detrimental effects, if it does exist, is magnified simply because living organisms reproduce, often at very rapid rates. Other types of environmental stresses tend to be dissipated with time, but the potential harm from living organisms may spread and become increasingly severe.

Genetic Changes

It is frequently stated that the slight changes arising from genetic engineering will not alter the harmfulness of organisms. However, this view also does not conform with what we know about the behavior of microorganisms. Slight genetic changes, admittedly induced in the era before genetic engineering, do bring about major modifications in the potential harmfulness of some microorganisms . . .

Similarly, the influenza virus presumably undergoes regular genetic changes in nature, and these genetic changes lead to the widespread dissemination of the virus, frequently with an enormous number of human deaths; here, the selective advantage of the new genotype is not obvious. It is difficult to see why a man-made genetic change would necessarily behave any differently from those occurring spontaneously in nature: it too could proliferate, spread, and do harm to susceptible humans, animals, plants, or microorganisms important to natural environmental functions.

Disasters arising from introduced microorganisms are well known to epidemiologists, animal scientists, and plant pathologists. The microorganism causing the Dutch elm disease in a few years nearly wiped out the population of susceptible trees. A single microbial species is estimated to have eliminated most chestnuts from 50,000,000 acres of the United States in but a few years. In the 1970s, a fungus spread rapidly through the corn crop of the United States, and the disease induced is estimated to have reduced the corn yield in this country by 10 percent, clearly a major impact. A virus deliberately introduced into Australia nearly wiped out the rabbit population of that country. Influenza affects many humans each year, but when a new genetic variant of the influenza virus appeared in 1918, millions of people were killed. It has also been estimated that the microorganism causing smallpox killed more than 95 percent of the native Indians of Mexico, and that about 90 percent of the natives of Hawaii died because of the introduction of new microorganisms into the islands. In most but not all such instances, the microorganisms did not represent new genotypes, but rather they were organisms that moved to a new environment. The reason I cite these well known epidemiological facts is to illustrate that a microorganism that has the capacity to survive and grow, if it makes contact with an appropriate host, may spread rapidly through the host population and cause disastrous changes.

It is thus my view that alien organisms that are inadvertently or deliberately introduced into natural environments may survive, they may grow, they may find a susceptible host or other environment, and they may do harm. I believe that the probability of all these events occurring is small, but I feel that it is likely that the consequences of this low-probability event may be enormous . . .

The prudent course of action is to establish the risk factors and simultaneously develop a regulatory procedure to assess survival, growth, and deleterious effects. Assessments of potential survival and growth can be done at modest cost. Procedures do not now exist to measure deleterious effects of microorganisms on natural populations at low cost, but there has not been a significant amount of research to develop such procedures. In this way, we may gain the many benefits of genetic engineering while not being exposed to the likely hazards from the misuse of the technology.

ENVIRONMENTAL BENEFITS OF GENETIC ENGINEERING

Ananda Chakrabarty

Dr. Ananda Chakrabarty is a research biologist with the Department of Microbiology at the University of Illinois Medical Center in Chicago. He developed the first living micro-organism to receive a U.S. federal patent. In the Supreme Court case Diamond v Chakrabarty, 447 US 303 (1980), the high court ruled that living organisms were patentable in a five to four decision.

Points to Consider

1. What guidelines now cover research procedures in genetic manipulation of bacteria?
2. How will genetic manipulation of bacteria help improve the environment?
3. What are the health hazards posed by toxic chemical pollution?
4. Why are guidelines needed to regulate the release of micro-organisms into the open environment?

Excerpted from testimony by Ananda Chakrabarty before the House Subcommittee on Science, Research and Technology, 1983.

There are reasons why we might be interested in deliberately releasing genetically manipulated bacteria in an open environment.

I would like to thank all of you for giving me this opportunity to express my views before this august body on topics related to the use of genetically engineered micro-organisms in an open environment.

As you are all aware, there are specific guidelines stipulated by NIH that dictate the level of physical or biological containment in the preparation and large-scale production of useful drugs and pharmaceuticals such as insulin, human growth hormone, interferon, et cetera. Production of such bacteria, and the level of their accidental release in an open environment, can be stringently controlled by appropriate physical containment. There are, however, other reasons why we might be interested in deliberately releasing genetically manipulated bacteria in an open environment. I will illustrate this point by giving you examples of research areas that we are pursuing at the University of Illinois at Chicago which will necessitate the application of any micro-organism we develop in an open environment.

The first one is the area of toxic chemical pollution. Undoubtedly, you are aware of the potential health hazards posed by the presence of a large number of toxic chemical dumpsites all over the country. Many of the buried drums containing the toxic chemicals get corroded over a long period of time, and the released chemicals move downward to contaminate the aquifers from which we derive our drinking water or move up and contaminate the surface, leading to poisoning of human beings and animals.

In addition, deliberate or inadvertent release of toxic chemicals often leads to human contamination—as the cases in Love Canal, Seveso, and Times Beach will exemplify.

Unfortunately, we have no technology that allows purification of contaminated soil, so that the only thing we can do is to ban the production or usage of the chemicals and evacuate people from the contaminated areas. This, of course, does not address the problem of how to get rid of the chemicals from the area of contamination.

Since micro-organisms traditionally have been responsible for recycling the natural wastes and maintaining the carbon, nitrogen, and sulfur cycle in nature, it is the inability of the natural micro-flora to biodegrade synthetic chemicals that has led to the present-day toxic chemical pollution problem.

102

Yet, I feel that microbial genetic engineering can play a role in solving some of these problems. As an example, I would like to cite the development in our laboratories of a bacterial strain that can utilize 2,4,5-T, a major component of agent orange, as a sole source of carbon and energy. This bacterium has been demonstrated to remove large concentrations of 2,4,5-T, 10,000 to 20,000 parts per million, from heavily contaminated soil within a few weeks. Removal of the 2,4,5-T allows the soil to support growth of broad-leaf plants, which are sensitive to the presence of low concentrations, let's say about 15 or 20 parts per million or less, of 2,4,5-T. Once the 2,4,5-T is gone, the bacteria die off within a few weeks, becoming undetectable after a couple of months. Since no naturally-occurring micro-organisms, pure or mixed, are known to utilize 2,4,5-T as a sole source of carbon, such experiments appear to raise hope that laboratory-developed bacterial strains may be effective in removing at least some of the priority toxic chemicals from the environment . . .

The commercial implications of using microbial technology for enhanced recovery of oil are enormous . . .

Specific Guidelines

There are, however, no specific guidelines that regulate the release of micro-organisms in an open environment, either for toxic chemical clean-up or oil recovery. Well-defined guidelines,

The Structure of DNA

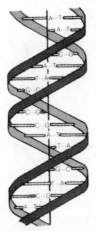 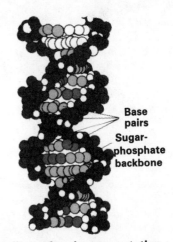

A schematic diagram of the DNA double helix.

A three-dimensional representation of the DNA double helix.

Base pairs
Sugar-phosphate backbone

The DNA molecule is a double helix composed of two chains. The sugar-phosphate backbones twist around the outside, with the paired bases on the inside serving to hold the chains together.
SOURCE: Office of Technology Assessment.

103

not necessarily legislation, would be very useful in allowing an evaluation of the effectiveness of this emerging microbial technology.

Recognizing that such research is being conducted by small companies, legislation to allow tax incentives for research and development in the area of energy and pollution control, and an expeditious review of application of genetically engineered micro-organisms and related products by regulatory agencies such as the Environmental Protection Agency, would be very helpful.

In addition, limited legal liability for the use of genetically engineered micro-organisms is, at least initially, a necessity to allow appropriate field trials to be conducted in toxic chemical dumpsite areas or oil well areas. I hope this hearing will form the basis to enable the committees to draw up a few of such guidelines.

COUNTERPOINTS

THE DANGERS OF BIOTECHNOLOGY: POINTS AND COUNTERPOINTS

Stephen R. Gliessman vs. Ralph W. Hardy

Stephen R. Gliessman is a biologist and agroecologist. He is currently an assistant professor of environmental studies and the director of the University of California agroecology program in Santa Cruz, California. Ralph W. Hardy is the Director of Life Sciences in the Central Research and Development Department of the Du Pont Company. He is also a member of the Committee on Genetic Experimentation of the International Council of Scientific Unions.

Points to Consider

1. What kind of experiment has the National Institute of Health given permission to carry out?
2. Why does Stephen Gliessman think present guidelines for research are not safe?
3. Why does Ralph W. Hardy think guidelines for research are safe?
4. Which argument do you agree with?

Stephen R. Gliessman in a public letter, 1983, and Ralph W. Hardy in testimony before the House Subcommittee on Science, Research and Technology, 1983.

THE POINT: by Stephen R. Gliessman

It is my understanding that the National Institutes of Health (NIH) has approved three experiments for the release of genetically engineered organisms into the environment. I also understand that these experiments have received the approval of the Recombinant DNA Advisory Committee (RAC). These are the first experiments in which genetically engineered living organisms have been released into the open environment. Such experimentation is being carried out without the assurance that certain risks may not be present for not only human health, but also for other animal or plant life. Present guidelines for testing possible long-term effects of such introductions are very incomplete. No actual procedures have been drawn up for testing the release of new life forms.

Ecological Concerns

As an ecologist working on agricultural systems, I have the following concerns:

a. The introduction of a novel or exotic life form into the environment can seriously upset the natural balance of the target ecosystem.

b. An introduction today, which at first seems to cause no problems, can take many years for the detrimental effects of its presence to be known, sometimes at a point where the reversal of the effects may be practically impossible.

c. The subtleties of the complex interactions between living organisms requires considerable ecological expertise in order to gain a full understanding of how they function. Current work with genetic engineering too often lacks any adequate ecological screening. This creates a void in our understanding of how such manipulated organisms will react once released into the open environment.

d. Manipulated or altered living organisms cannot be treated as merely a chemical substance, thus are not adequately covered by the present EPA Toxic Substances Control Act. Natural selection or adaptation once such organisms are released is frequently beyond human control.

e. Species displacement through niche overlap or competition with closely related organisms is very difficult to predict, but must be included as a possible outcome of introductions.

Conclusion

In conclusion, a federal agency (NIH) has given approval for experimentation with the release of genetically altered life forms into the environment without the establishment of proper protocol for determining potential ecological effects. A procedure for establishing proper Environmental Impact Reports for such organisms needs to be determined. Methodologies need to be devised and field tested before such experiments are carried out. Risk assessment which takes into account ecological parameters is of vital importance. Release of altered life forms should definitely be postponed until such procedures and methodologies are established.

THE COUNTERPOINT: by Ralph W. Hardy

Exciting as the advances which may be realized through biotechnology may be, we must also be cognizant of some potential safety and environmental quality concerns which could result from the application of these developing technologies. In order to assure that any potential hazards do not become reality, we recommend a controlled, stepwise, progressive program of development beginning in the laboratory and moving with deliberate caution through the plant growth room and greenhouse before finally entering limited field evaluations which can be closely supervised. Through such a programmed cautionary approach, we can maximize the scientific impacts while minimizing any unknown consequences for the environment. This stepwise approach is consistent with the NIH guidelines which were initially quite cautious and were revised to be consistent with experience.

At this time no health hazards have been identifed for personnel involved with biotechnology research. With plant research involving recombinant DNA techniques carried out under the NIH guidelines we feel that adequate standards of safety can be maintained for the worker.

Original Concerns

The original concerns voiced about recombinant DNA research were based on projected consequences of release of new organisms into the environment. These include the potential for release of new plant pests which might cause devastation to agronomically important species. Such organisms could be plant or microorganism species which might find an ecological niche and be difficult to control. By using the controlled developmental approach outlined above, and operating under the NIH guidelines established for recombinant DNA research, such deleterious consequences should be avoided. As an example, if a new potentially useful plant species were developed in the laboratory but subsequently found to be a potential pest such as a weed when released into a specific environmental situation, ade-

107

quate control measures such as herbicides are available to destroy the new species so that it would not gain an uncontrolled foothold and adversely affect the ecosystem. Such early recognition, planning and control would avoid environmental consequences such as those now being realized as a result of the introduction of the kudzu vine for erosion control in Southeastern U.S.

With the development of novel microorganisms through the application of the techniques of molecular genetics a more cautious approach may be necessary since it is more difficult to recall or control microorganisms than plants.

This will require extended periods of laboratory, growth room, and greenhouse testing under varying simulated environmental conditions prior to actual field testing. Such a controlled approach to beneficial applications of the results of new recombinant DNA technology can be adequately covered through the existing oversight mechanisms contained in the NIH guidelines . . .

Many products of biotechnology in the agricultural and health care area will require demonstration of safety and/or efficacy prior to marketing. This may require several years. Extension of patent life to make up for the years required to meet regulatory requirements will encourage vigorous commercial searching and development of biotechnology products by U.S. industry.

Conclusion

In conclusion, let me say that biotechnology research is moving at a rapid pace with new exciting practical applications beginning to emerge. This field has immense potential to benefit mankind. It is relatively low risk for those directly involved in the scientific efforts, for the general population, and for the environment. Adequate controls and safeguards are provided through existing guidelines and administrative regulations. We must foster advancement of biotechnology through training a cadre of new scientists in our universities and by providing incentives for industry to bring the results of the basic scientific discoveries to practical application.

EXAMINING COUNTERPOINTS

This activity may be used as an individualized study guide for students in libraries and resource centers or as a discussion catalyst in small group and classroom discussions.

The Point

With the arrival of genetic engineering, it will soon be possible to engineer and produce human beings by the same technological design principles as we now employ in our industrial processes.

The Counterpoint

The idea that it will be possible to successfully and directly engineer and design complex human traits in any foreseeable future is simply preposterous. The human genetic universe is simply too complicated for any notions like that.

●   ●   ●   ●   ●   ●

The Point

Human genetic engineering offers the promise of overthrowing the tyrants of human disease and new commercial opportunities.

The Counterpoint

Human genetic engineering presents the twin perils of possible ecological catastrophies and the moral disasters of new human life forms created in the laboratory.

109

Guidelines

Part A

Examine the counterpoints above and then consider the following questions.

1. Do you agree more with the point or the counterpoint in each case? Why?

2. Which reading in this book best illustrates the first point? Which best illustrates the first counterpoint?

3. Which reading best illustrates the second point? Which best illustrates the second counterpoint?

4. Do any cartoons in this publication illustrate the meaning of the point or counterpoint arguments? Which ones and why?

Part B

Social issues are usually complex, but often problems become oversimplified in political debates and discussions. Usually a polarized version of social conflict does not adequately represent the diversity of views that surround social conflicts. Examine the counterpoints above. Then write down other possible interpretations of genetic engineering than the ones stated in the counterpoints.

CHAPTER 5

SPLICING DEATH: THE GLOBAL THREAT OF BIOLOGICAL WAR

A MONSTER WAKES IN THE WORLD'S LABS

John Hubner

John Hubner is a columnist and political commentator for the Knight-Ridder News Service. In the following article he outlines the new threats of biological warfare presented to humanity by the revolutionary developments in the science of bio-engineering.

Points to Consider

1. What kind of weapons could be developed using recombinant DNA technology?
2. Why are fears on the rise about biological warfare?
3. What kind of research in biological weapons is being conducted by the U.S. Defense Department?
4. What is the "most basic question of all?"

John Hubner, "A Monster Wakes in the World's Labs," Knight-Ridder News Service, 1984.

You could take a disease like smallpox that we have all but eradicated, genetically alter it to make it resistant to vaccination, clandestinely release the virus and create a horrid epidemic.

Thinking the unthinkable.

The phrase brings to mind images of the lieutenant who trails the president with the black box, or of uniformed men sitting around a table deep in the Pentagon, devising nuclear war games. Sad to say, the unthinkable has new meaning these days. We have more to fear than nuclear war.

Today, some scientists and military men are bringing back to life a Frankenstein monster. The beast is sitting up, rubbing its eyes. Are we on the verge of an arms race in chemical and biological weapons?

"The menace to international security from CBW (chemical and biological warfare) developments during previous years has become more evident . . . Increased military preparedness for CBW may soon accelerate, irreversibly, into a grotesque new arms race. The prospect then may be one of CBW weapons becoming 'conventional': poised for use wherever and whenever military necessities may be satisfied by their special properties."

"Generals say, 'Oh, a CBW attack would wipe out the forces in the first 20 minutes. We couldn't have our war games,'" said Dr. William Beisel, deputy director for science at the U.S. Army Medical Research Institute for Infectious Diseases (USAMRIID) in Fort Detrick, Md.

What's more, there are strong international prohibitions against CBW. The 1925 Geneva Protocol outlawed the use (though not the stockpiling) of chemical weapons. The 1972 Biological Weapons Convention banned the use of biological weapons and was the first treaty in modern times that actually resulted in the destruction of stockpiled weapons.

So why is the Department of Defense spending $100 million a year to develop medical defenses against chemical warfare and $30 million a year for medical defenses against biological warfare? What has changed since 1972?

There is a one-word answer to these questions: bio-engineering. This new field makes possible genetically engineered weapons that could revolutionize warfare the way the atomic bomb did 40 years ago. Advances in biotechnology have made the CBW threat so potent the military cannot ignore it.

"Unless we do something to keep the technology out of the military arena now, while it is still in its infancy, we won't be

Recombinant DNA: The Technique of Recombining Genes From One Species With Those of Another

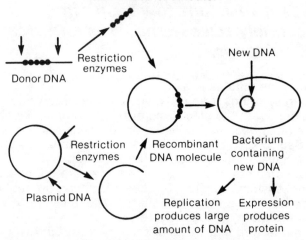

Restriction enzymes recognize certain sites along the DNA and can chemically cut the DNA at those sites. This makes it possible to remove selected genes from donor DNA molecules and insert them into plasmid DNA molecules to form the recombinant DNA. This recombinant DNA can then be cloned in its bacterial host and large amounts of a desired protein can be produced.

SOURCE: Office of Technology Assessment.

able to," said Dr. Robert Sinsheimer, a former California Scientist of the Year who is chancellor of University of California-Santa Cruz.

If you have read anything about bio-engineering, you know the new science is our best hope to cure cancer and hereditary diseases. Recombinant DNA technology does at the gene level what grafting does for fruit trees. Scientists use Escherichia coli (E. coli), a species of bacteria found in the human intestine, as tiny biological factories. The human gene for insulin, for example, is grafted onto E. coli, the bacteria are placed in a fermentation tank and the tiny bugs make insulin.

CBW agents are cheap, and they do not destroy property. Biotechnology makes it possible to manufacture bugs and gas that are deadlier than ever, and to do it faster than ever. Say you wanted to wipe out an army, a city or even a whole society—here are some of your options:

• You could take a disease like smallpox that we have all but eradicated, genetically alter it to make it resistant to vaccination, clandestinely release the virus and create a horrid epidemic.

114

- You could release a virus created through genetic engineering that was unknown to enemy doctors, but for which your doctors have developed a vaccine. Make it fast-acting, release it on a large scale.
- Starting with a rare virus like diphtheria, you could use recombinant DNA techniques to graft it to the common E. coli and make a devastating weapon, particularly if you had vaccinated your troops against diphtheria before releasing it.
- You could use biotech to make chemical warfare possible. Generals traditionally have disliked poison gases because they are dangerous to use. Even the best protective clothing doesn't guarantee your soldiers won't suffer as badly as the enemy's. But if you could inoculate your troops against nerve gas, say, so that it wouldn't harm them even if they inhaled it, you would have a weapon as deadly and selective as a bullet.
- You could make deadly viruses more deadly. Botulism, for instance, only grows in a dark environment. Using the new technology, however, you could extract the plasmid sensitive to sunlight, improve its ultraviolet resistance and make it tough enough to reproduce in daylight.
- You could target victims by skin color. Some races are more susceptible to certain diseases than other races. San Joaquin Valley fever, for example—for which a vaccine is being developed at a Navy lab in Oakland, Calif.—is much more deadly to dark-skinned people than to Caucasians. Suppose South Africa and Zimbabwe were at war. Releasing valley fever would be the perfect way for South Africa to soften its enemy without too much threat to its white soldiers.

Then there's the possibility of using CBW against civilians. A century ago, dozens of varieties of corn were grown in America. Today, because of the development of fast-growing, high-yield hybrids, six varieties of corn produce 70 percent of the U.S. crop. If an enemy developed a fungus that attacked only the half-dozen varieties of corn grown in the United States, it could wipe out a major underpinning of the American economy.

Fear on the Rise

Fear about this sort of thing is on the rise. In 1981, Cuba claimed a clandestine U.S. operation was responsible for a major outbreak of dengue fever that occurred between May and October of that year.

Dengue is an acute infectious disease caused by the bite of the Aedes mosquito, the same insect that transmits yellow fever. Victims suffer through several days of fever, headaches and such pain in the joints that the disease was once called "breakbone." There have been other dengue epidemics in the South

Knowledge For Evil

Once again we confront the age-old problem: Can we prevent the misuse of human knowledge for evil purpose? Can we forestall the perversion of human ingenuity to the depravity of war? Archimedes used his knowledge of mechanics to design catapults. Leonardo applied his genius to the invention of engines of war. The scientists of Los Alamos developed the atomic bomb. Is the new synthetic biology likewise to be the source of new and dreadful weapons?

Deliberate construction of harmful biological agents has generally been acknowledged as the most extreme biohazard associated with recombinant DNA technology.

Susan Wright and Robert L. Sinsheimer, *Bulletin of Atomic Scientists,* 1983

and the Caribbean, but none so serious as the one that struck Cuba.

The 1981 outbreak was the first epidemic on the island since 1944. The cases came from three widely separated parts of Cuba. More than 300,000 cases were reported; at the height of the epidemic, there were 10,000 new cases a day. One hundred fifty-eight people died, 101 of them children under the age of 15.

In blaming the United States, Cuban officials claimed it was unlikely that the disease had broken out spontaneously in three spots at the same time; that there were no reports of the disease in the Bahamas and Jamaica, and only 22 cases in Haiti; that none of the early victims had ever been off the island, and that none had been away from home in the weeks before the outbreak occurred.

Research Projects

The grant is only $100,000, but it is one of the most important of the Defense Department's $100 million chemical defense research projects. It is being conducted by John Baxter at the University of California-San Francisco biochemistry laboratory.

Baxter is using recombinant DNA techniques to clone the human gene for acetylcholinesterase, an important neurotransmitter that is involved in half of the body's synapses. It is the body's on-off switch, starting the electrochemical reaction that stimulates a muscle, turning the synapsis off when the function is complete. Organophosphorus, the deadly ingredient in nerve gases, attacks acetylcholinesterase, causing it to lock in the "on" position. A nerve gas victim's entire nervous system fires simultaneously, like a box of firecrackers exploding at once, until the victim overstimulates to death. You've seen it happen if you've ever sprayed a cockroach with insecticide and watched it writhe and die.

Across the bay on the Oakland waterfront is the military's major biological lab on the West Coast, the Naval Biosciences Laboratory. A UC-Berkeley facility under contract to the Office of Naval Research, the lab employs 100 people and has a $4.2 million annual budget, 85 percent of which comes from the military. Its director is Dr. David Kingsbury, a professor at the university's School of Public Health. Among other projects, the lab is studying the genetics of bubonic plague, making a vaccine for San Joaquin Valley fever and producing monoclonal antibodies for highly contagious diseases like Lassa and Rift Valley fevers.

The U.S. Army Medical Research Institute for Infectious Diseases has headquarters in Fort Detrick, an hour or so north of Washington, D.C., in Frederick, Md. Inside the institute building, technicians wearing blue space suits attached to yellow air hoses are working with the most lethal organisms known, exotic killers like botulism, anthrax, Rift Valley fever, dengue fever, Lassa and Korean hemorrhagic fevers, and rickettsial diseases.

Fort Detrick was the headquarters of America's biological warfare program from 1942 until 1969, when President Nixon issued an executive order unilaterally stopping the researching and stockpiling of biological weapons.

From 1969 through the '70s, most of the research that went on at Fort Detrick was conducted by the National Cancer Institute. In 1979, the military recognized both the promise and the threat posed by biotechnology and reopened the laboratories.

"None of the work we are doing here is aimed at developing an offensive biological weapons capability," says Dr. William Beisel, the overseer of the $30 million Defense Department biological research program. "The Defense Department is not developing an offensive biological warfare capability, is not doing research to create new toxins or make existing diseases more toxic."

In October 1950, the Army blanketed the San Francisco area with a micro-organism called Serratia marcescens. The Army was afraid that the Russians might secretly attack us with lethal bacteria; they wanted to find how and where the bugs would drift into the lungs of unsuspecting citizens. The Army considered the micro-organism harmless, but later tests implicated it in several illnesses and at least one death.

"How do we know they won't do it again?" asked Jonathan King, a microbiologist at the Massachusetts Institute of Technology.

The possibility of secret testing is not the only reason critics feel the military—as opposed to, say, the National Institutes of Health—might not be the most appropriate agency to fund biotech research. Suppose, for example, the Army successfully develops new vaccines for shigellosis and Rift Valley fever, diseases that have paralyzed Third World countries.

Most Basic Question

Then, we come back to the most basic queston of all. Are the military's CBW researchers creating an arms race in chemical and biological weapons?

Scientists think of science as a natural force, like gravity. You can't stop it; you are foolish to try. The scientist lives to make discoveries; how those discoveries are used is society's concern.

But some scientists are abandoning this traditional position of amoral neutrality to question the Defense Department's use of biotechnology in the CBW defense program. They point out that the military isn't just in the business of making vaccines to protect soldiers. It is also in the business of learning to kill people as quickly and efficiently as possible. Biotechnology is seductive because it offers new and better ways to do that.

Suppose we had known 40 years ago what we know now about nuclear technology—about the unending flood of apocalyptic weaponry it would produce. Would we have accepted this kind of assurance and said, "Go ahead"? Or would we have done everything we could to stop nuclear weapons before they were ever developed?

The choice is ours—but it may not be for long.

BIOLOGICAL WAR: THE U.S. THREAT

Jeremy Rifkin

Jeremy Rifkin is the founder and director of the Foundation on Economic Trends (1346 Connecticut Avenue N.W., Suite 1010, Washington, D.C. 20036). He is the author of Algeny, *a critique of the emerging biotechnical society. His many speeches and articles warn of the moral and environmental dangers he thinks are presented by human genetic engineering. Mr. Rifkin appeared before the Recombinant DNA Advisory Committee (RAC) of the National Institute of Health (NIH). These federal bodies set up guidelines for research in genetic engineering.*

Points to Consider

1. Why is Mr. Rifkin opposed to the cloning of the Shiga toxin?
2. What kind of research is the Department of Defense (DOD) doing?
3. What distinctions are made between offensive and defensive research in biological warfare?
4. What does Mr. Rifkin say to the committee about crimes against humanity?

Excerpted from a statement by Jeremy Rifkin before the Recombinant DNA Advisory Committee of the National Institute of Health, 1982.

Experiments like the kind being considered today could be used to advance the knowledge of how to develop biological weapons as well.

We are formally requesting that the Recombinant DNA Advisory Committee (RAC) of the National Institutes of Health (NIH) table indefinitely any action on the proposal to clone a Shiga toxin . . .

Present and former members of the RAC have, on several occasions, noted that recombinant DNA experiments being conducted by the various branches of the Armed Services have the "potential" to be used in slightly altered or modified form for the purposes of weapons development. Such weapons development would be in violation of the 1972 Treaty unconditionally banning biological warfare experimentation. Writing in the November 1983 edition of the **Bulletin of Atomic Scientists,** Robert J. Sinzheimer, a renouned biophysicist, and chancellor of the University of California at Santa Cruz observed that because of the nature of this particular category of experimentation, there is no adequate way to properly distinguish between peaceful uses of deadly toxins and military uses. According to Sinzheimer, experiments like the kind being considered today could be used to advance the knowledge of how to develop biological weapons as well.

No Difference Between Offense and Defense

The DOD points out that many of the DNA related experiments it is engaged in are designed to produce useful vaccines. Yet even here, many scientists working in the field agree that much of this type of experimentation advances the knowledge that could be easily used for weapons development. According to the Stockholm International Peace Research Institute's exhaustive study on chemical and biological warfare, while "the typical vaccine plant is inadequate for the production of a full military capability it would be adequate for the production of quantities (of biological warfare agents) required for a sabotage attack . . . Some common forms of vaccine production are very close technically to production of CBW agents and so offer easy opportunities for conversion." Col. Richard Barquist, who heads the U.S. Army Medical Research Institute of Infectious Diseases apparently concurs with this assessment. In a recent interview with the Associated Press, Col. Barquist said "as far as (recombinant DNA) research goes, there's no difference (between offense and defense)."

120

Former RAC member Dr. Richard Goldstein, professor of microbiology of Harvard Medical School, sums up the nature of these kinds of biological experiments currently being conducted by the DOD. Under the banner of defensive purposes, the DOD "can justify working with the super pathogens of the world—producing altered and more virulent strains, producing vaccines for protection of their troops against such agents . . . and likewise for the development of dispersal systems since DOD must be able to defend against any such dispersal system. Under this guise, what DOD ends up with is a new biological weapon system—a virulent organism, a vaccine against it, and a dispersal system. As you can gather from this, there is but a very thin

PROBABLE ENEMY METHODS OF DELIVERING BIOLOGICAL AGENTS

AIRCRAFT SPRAY

AERIAL BOMBLETS

BOMBLETS FROM MISSILES

ROCKETS

VECTORS

COVERT/SABOTAGE

Biological Warfare

Biological warfare goes back at least to medieval times, when combatants occasionally threw animal carcasses—and accompanying diseases—into the camps of besieged enemies. The merchants of death have grown much more sophisticated since then, and today they have a new technology to draw on: recombinant DNA.

Though the United States is a signatory to the Biological Weapons Convention of 1972, the Government apparently has plans to include genetically altered organisms in its arsenal. This can theoretically be done in the name of defense, since the Convention prohibits the development only of bacterial and biological weapons "that have no justification for prophylactic, protective, or other peaceful purposes."

The Progressive Editorial, 1983

line—if any—between such a defensive system (allowed by the convention) and any prohibited offensive system."

The point is, members of RAC, advisors to RAC, other prominent scientists and military experts agree that experiments like the proposed Shiga experiment being considered today are technologies "with potential military application or weapons systems applications" and therefore are subject to section 36 (a)(3) of the Arms Control and Disarmament Act. It is my understanding that the DOD and the Arms Control and Disarmament Agency are in non-compliance with this act in regard to the Shiga experiment and other biological experiments involving recombinant DNA technology. Therefore, it would be improper for the RAC to consider this proposed experiment to clone a Shiga toxin until such time as a weapons impact statement covering this experiment and/or the category of experiments it is part of, is forthcoming from the Arms Control and Disarmament Agency.

Crimes Against Humanity

Moreover, I would remind this committee that in authorizing this and other related DOD experiments involving DNA technology and toxins it is, defacto, acting in complicity with the Arms Control and Disarmament Agency in violation of section 36 of the Arms Control and Disarmament Act which requires a weapons impact statement for the development of any technology with "potential military applications." I should also remind the committee that if this experiment or any other experiment authorized by RAC is later modified and used for the specific purpose of developing and employing biological warfare weapons, each member of this committee would be personally liable under international law and the principles enunciated at Nuremberg in aiding in the commission of a crime against humanity.

It will not suffice for members of this committee to wash their hands of any responsibility for how the knowledge gained in these types of experiments will be subsequently used. In authorizing the Shiga experiment and other similar experiments, this committee becomes an active participant in the final uses to which this work is put.

For that reason, I urge this committee to place a moratorium on all further authorizations of DOD related toxin experiments until such time as this committee engages in a full dialogue with all other interested agencies in the Executive and Congressional branches relative to the potential uses of this technology for biological warfare purposes.

According to the National Science Foundation, expenditures on all biological research by the DOD have increased 54% since 1980 reaching $100 million in 1983. I urge everyone on this committee to peruse the annual reports on Biological Programs submitted to Congress by the military from 1980 to 1983. I believe that many members of this committee might well entertain second thoughts about the long term potential use and abuse of DNA experimentation upon close reading of the mushrooming number of so-called "defensive" programs being launched by the various military branches.

The fact is, we have known for several years now that recombinant DNA technology is a powerful tool: one that could be used for mass destructive purposes.

All of these warning signals suggest that a full review of DOD experiments using recombinant DNA technology is in order. I hope this committee will take the opportunity today to halt all further involvement with DOD related experiments in this field pending an arms control weapons impact study (ACIS) and a thorough review by the RAC and NIH of the degree to which it would like to be involved in the process of authorizing experiments like the cloning of Shiga toxin.

BIOLOGICAL WAR:
THE SOVIET THREAT

Les Aspin and Mark Popovskiy

*Les Aspin is a democratic congressman from Wisconsin.
Mark Popovskiy is an emigre from the Soviet Union and
Fellow at the Kennan Institute for Advanced Russian
Studies of the Smithsonian's Woodrow Wilson
International Center for Scholars.*

Points to Consider

1. Why was the Biological Weapons Convention of 1972 unique?
2. What specifically did the Biological Weapons Convention state?
3. What does Mr. Popovskiy say the Soviets are doing in Sverdlovsk?
4. What does he say the explosion at Sverdlovsk signifies?

Excerpted from testimony by Les Aspin and Mark Popovskiy before the
House Committee on Intelligence, 1980.

For a long time now there has existed in Sverdlovsk a secret military compound working on bacteriological weapons.

Statement by Les Aspin

In 1972, the United States and the Soviet Union signed the Biological Weapons Convention which outlaws the development, production, or stockpiling of biological warfare agents. The convention went into effect in 1975, and it has been ratified now by 112 nations, a multilateral convention.

The Biological Weapons Convention is unique among all contemporary arms control agreements because it is not built around an effective verification scheme. Even though the convention does have sections that lay out procedures to be followed in case of a violation, the convention was negotiated in full knowledge that there was no way to assure compliance.

Bacteriological weapons, just by their very nature, can be produced in small laboratories, so even if the signatories to the convention began with total knowledge of each other's facilities, and even if it could be demonstrated that all stocks of bacteriological warfare agents had been destroyed and production facilities closed down, there still could be no assurance that covert production might not get underway in some form. It is a very, very difficult thing to monitor.

The drafters of the convention relied for safety on two major assumptions. One was the lack of very good utility of biological weapons. Military planners in the United States were unenthusiastic about biological warfare since it posed tremendous uncertainties in application and might backfire disastrously on friendly forces and territories.

There was a sense that the United States had no need for these weapons and if they were ever used against us, there were other ways to retaliate. I think that we went into that agreement feeling that common sense would indicate that it was not a very effective or a very useful form of warfare.

The second factor was that U.S. arms controllers reasoned that any effort by the Soviet Union to conceal a substantial biological warfare capability might eventually misfire in a way that would tip us off. The political consequences of such an event would, it was thought, be of such magnitude as to convince any rational Soviet leader that the risks outweighed the gain.

So in spite of the fact that there was no really good way to verify that convention, it was thought that these two factors were enough, perhaps, to make sure that the convention was complied with.

Last March, the Biological Warfare Convention had its review. When the convention went into effect in 1975, article 12 provided that:

Five years after entry into force of this convention, a conference of states parties to the convention shall be held in Geneva, Switzerland to review the operation of the convention with a view to assuring that the purposes of the preamble and the provisions of the convention are being realized.

That conference was held in Geneva during the first 3 weeks of March 1980. Three days before the conference ended, the United States raised the matter of allegations that an anthrax epidemic related to biological weapons had broken out in Sverdlovsk, and the conference also discussed proposals for strengthening the verification of the convention.

It is important to realize what the convention states and what it doesn't state. The Biological Warfare Convention obligated signatory states not to "develop, produce, stockpile, or otherwise acquire or retain biological agents of types or in quantities that have no justification for prophylactic, protective, or other peaceful purposes."

Whether the accident in Sverdlovsk demonstrates that the Soviets are producing or retaining stockpiles of anthrax in quantities excessive for peaceful uses, such as the development of vaccines, or testing defensive measures against biological warfare by other countries is thus a question that remains to be answered before any judgment that the Soviet Union is in violation of the 1975 convention.

What we are saying is that any judgment that the Soviet Union has violated the 1975 convention thus depends on the answer to the following question: Does the anthrax in Sverdlovsk demonstrate that the Soviets are producing or retaining a stockpile of anthrax in quantities excessive for peaceful use or for testing defensive measures against the possibility of biological warfare by other countries?

Statement by Mark Popovskiy

As a writer who had written in the U.S.S.R. between 1947 and 1977 on men and problems of science, I had learned the following facts from my conversations with scientists.

One: For a long time now there has existed in Sverdlovsk a secret military compound working on bacteriological weapons.

Two: This compound is part of a system working on the development and testing of bacteriological weapons, and it consists of several institutes and field test sites. I know specifically of two such institutes in the cities of Kirov and Sverdlovsk. I

126

know that the Soviet army general staff has a special seventh section, specializing in the development and testing of bacteriological weapons and vaccines, which for many years has been headed, that is section No. 7, headed by Colonel General—which is equivalent to a three star general in the U.S. Army—Efim Ivanovich Smirnov. The medical work is under the direction of U.S.S.R. Deputy Minister of Health Burgasov—that is the name of the deputy minister—who works in close cooperation with the KGB. At least until recently, 125 microbiologists, epidemiologists, zoologists, and specialists on communicable diseases worked at the secret bacteriological compound in Kirov—that's the town—which is surrounded by two rows of concrete walls. Plague, tularemia, tetanus, anthrax, and yellow fever were some of the infectious diseases worked on by Soviet experts at these secret compounds.

Three: Knowing all this, and the fact that military bacteriological research had been carried on in the U.S.S.R. since the 1920's in the towns of Saratov, Suzdal, Moscow, Novosibirsk, and possibly Kalinin, I was not at all surprised when in February I received a letter through the underground sent to me from Moscow in January, in which a friend informed me that last spring an infectious strain had spread throughout Sverdlovsk, following an explosion in a secret bacteriological compound. My friend informed me that an infectious cloud had been driven by wind

127

south from the city, and that no less than 1,000 people had died, both in the city and its suburbs. Residents within a very large radius of the military bacteriological compound were vaccinated twice. The vaccinations were painful and people refused to go to the clinics for vaccination. The nature of the disease was not known, but it was thought to be a very virulent form of anthrax. Those who came down with the disease died within a few hours after arriving at the hospital.

Four: As far as I am concerned, the validity of these facts is unquestionable. In my books published in the U.S.S.R., I even described, indirectly, the bacteriological research carried out for military purposes without mentioning specifically where they had been carried out.

Five: On the basis of a large number of facts which were at my disposal in the U.S.S.R., I maintain that the Soviet Union never, either after 1925 or after 1975, carried out its commitment to renounce bacteriological weapons.

Venoms And Neurotoxins

As one assembles the evidence on Soviet genetic engineering, the picture of a program to develop new biological weapons emerges like a ghoulish jigsaw puzzle. Emigre scientists say their colleagues in the Soviet Union were already at work on such projects in the mid-1970s. A review of the open scientific literature confirms a heavy emphasis on snake venoms and other neurotoxins, especially in numerous articles by Academy of Sciences Vice President Yuri Ovchinnikov, identified by the emigres as the moving force behind the military program.

Recent Soviet military literature, meanwhile, describes how advances in genetic engineering have made biological weapons more effective and specifically how neurotoxins can be used in combat or for sabotage.

William Kucewics, *The Wall Street Journal*, May 18, 1984.

RECOGNIZING AUTHOR'S POINT OF VIEW

This activity may be used as an individualized study guide for students in libraries and resource centers or as a discussion catalyst in small group and classroom discussions.

The capacity to recognize an author's point of view is an essential reading skill. Many readers do not make clear distinctions between descriptive articles that relate factual information and articles that express a point of view. Think about the readings in chapters four and five. Are these readings essentially descriptive articles that relate factual information or articles that attempt to persuade through editorial commentary and analysis?

Guidelines

1. The following are brief descriptions of sources that appeared in chapters four and five. Choose one of the following source descriptions that best defines each source in chapters four and five.

Source Descriptions

a. Essentially an article that relates factual information
b. Essentially an article that expresses editorial points of view
c. Both of the above
d. Neither of the above

Sources in Chapters Four and Five

_____ Source Fourteen
"Biotechnology and the Environment: An Overview" by Albert Gore.

_____ Source Fifteen
"Environmental Risks of Genetic Engineering" by Martin Alexander.

_____ Source Sixteen
"Environmental Benefits of Genetic Engineering" by Ananda Chakrabarty.

_____ Source Seventeen
"The Dangers of Biotechnology: Points and Counterpoints" by Stephen R. Gliessman vs. Ralph W. Hardy.

_____ Source Eighteen
"A Monster Wakes in the World's Labs" by John Hubner.

_____ Source Nineteen
"Biological War: The U.S. Threat" by Jeremy Rifkin.
_____ Source Twenty
"Biological War: The Soviet Threat" by Les Aspin and
Mark Popovskiy.

2. Summarize the author's point of view in one to three sentences for each of the readings in chapters four and five.

3. After careful consideration, pick out one reading that you
   think is the most reliable source. Be prepared to explain the
   reasons for your choice in a general class discussion.

BIBLIOGRAPHY

INTRODUCTION

Biotechnology: A Review and Annotated Bibliography. Technology Policy Unit, University of Aston, Birmingham; prepared by Harry Rothman [et al.] (New York: Pergamon Press, 1981) 141 p.

Davies, Julian. "What's News in Biotechnology?" **Nature,** v. 299 (Oct. 7, 1982) pp. 493–496.

Judson, Horace Freeland. "Annals of Science: DNA." **New Yorker,** v. 54, (Nov. 27, Dec. 4, and Dec. 11, 1978).

Recombinant DNA. **Environment,** v. 24 (July-Aug. 1982) whole issue.

Recombinant DNA: Readings from Scientific American. With introductions by David Freifelder. (San Francisco: W. H. Freeman, 1978) 147 p.

Scott, Andrew. "Genetic Engineering: The Reconstruction of Animals and Plants." **New Scientist,** v. 95 (Aug. 26, 1982) pp. 562–564.

U.S. Congress. House. Committee on Science and Technology. Subcommittee on Science, Research, and Technology. Science Policy Implications of DNA Recombinant Molecule Research; Report. (Washington: U.S. Govt. Print. Off., 1978) 78 p.

U.S. Congress. Office of Technology Assessment. Impacts of Applied Genetics: Microorganisms, Plants, and Animals. (Washington: For sale by the Supt. of Docs., U.S. Govt. Print. Off., 1981) 331 p.

U.S. Library of Congress. Science Policy Research Division. Genetic Engineering: Evolution of a technological Issue. Report to the Subcommittee on Science, Research, and Development of the Committee on Science and Astronautics, U.S. House of Representatives, 92d Cong., 2d sess. (Washington: U.S. Govt. Print. Off., 1972) 119 p. Also Supplemental Reports I, II, and III.

Watson, James D. The DNA Story: A Documentary History of Gene Cloning, by James D. Watson and John Tooze. (San Francisco: W. H. Freeman, 1981) 605 p.

Watson, James D. **The Double Helix; a Personal Account of the Discovery of the Structure of DNA.** (New York: Atheneum, 1968) 226 p.

ETHICAL ISSUES

Adelman, Cynthia Smith. "The Constitutionality of Mandatory Genetic Screening Statutes." **Case Western Reserve Law Review,** v. 31 (Summer 1981) pp. 897–948.

Blank, Robert H. "Human Genetic Technology: Some Political Implications." **Social Science Journal,** v. 16 (Oct. 1979) pp. 1–19.

Bowman, James E. "Genetic Screening Programs and Public Policy." **Phylon,** v. 38, (June 1977) pp. 117–142.

Carmen, Ira H. "The Constitution in the Laboratory: Recombinant DNA Research as "Free Expression." **Journal of Politics,** v. 43 (Aug. 1981) pp. 737–762.

Denselow, Janis. "GMAG and the Teenage Jackass." **New Scientist,** v. 95 (Aug. 26, 1982) pp. 558–561.

Edson, Lee. "Should Scientists 'Play God'?" **Across the Board,** v. 17 (Oct. 1980) pp. 6–14.

Ellison, Craig W. "Engineering Humans: Who is to Do What to Whom?" **Christianity Today,** v. 23 (Jan. 19, 1979) pp. 14–18.

Graham, Loren. "Biomedicine and the Politics of Science in the USSR." **Soviet Union,** v. 8 (1981) pp. 147–158.

Grobstein, Clifford. **A Double Image of the Double Helix: The Recombinant-DNA Debate.** (San Francisco: W. H. Freeman, 1979) 177 p. (A Series of books in biology).

Guthrie, R. H. "DNA Technology: Are We Ready?" **Law/Technology,** v. 13, no. 3 (1980) pp. 1–27.

Holden, Constance. "Looking at Genes in the Workplace." **Science,** v. 217 (July 23, 1982) pp. 336–337.

Korwek, Edward L. "The NIH Guidelines for Recombinant DNA Research and the Authority of FDA to Require Compliance with the Guidelines." **Food Drug Cosmetic Law Journal,** v. 35 (Nov. 1980) pp. 633–650.

Krimsky, Sheldon, Anne Baeck, and John Bolduc. Municipal and State Recombinant DNA laws: History and Assessment. (Medford, Mass.: Tufts University, 1982) 1 v. (various pagings)

Lear, John. **Recombinant DNA: The Untold Story.** (New York: Crown Publishers, 1978) 280 p.

Lyman, Francesca. "New Life Forms for Fun and Profit." **Business and Society Review,** no. 40 (winter 1981–1982) pp. 40–44.

Morison, Robert S. Bioethics after Two Decades. **Hastings Center Report,** v. 11 (Apr. 1981) pp. 8–12.

Perpich, Joseph G. **Formulation of the NIH Guidelines for Recombinant DNA Research as an Exercise in Due Process.** In American Society of International Law. Proceedings of the 73rd annual meeting. [Washington, 1979] pp. 219–233.

Powledge, Tabitha M., and others. Recombinant DNA. **Hastings Center Report,** v. 7 (Apr. 1977) pp. 18–30.

The Recombinant DNA Debate. David A. Jackson and Stephen P. Stich, editors. (Englewood Cliffs, N.J.: Prentice-Hall, 1979) 385 p.

Rensberger, Boyce. "Tinkering with Life." **Science** 81, v. 2 (Nov. 1981) pp. 45–49.

Science and Public Interest: Recombinant DNA Research. Edited by Robert P. Bareikis. (Bloomington, Ind.: Poynter Center, 1978) 251 p.

Wright, Susan. "The Recombinant DNA Advisory Committee. "**Environment,** v. 21, (Apr. 1979) pp. 2–5, 40–41.

PATENTING LIFE FORMS

Bent, Stephen A. Patent Protection for DNA Molecules. **Journal of the Patent Office Society,** v. 64 (Feb. 1982) pp. 60–86.

Bloom, Allen. Designer Genes and Patent Law: a Good Fit. **New York Law School Law Review,** v. 24 (1981) pp. 1041–1057.

Brashear, James F. "Innocuous Inoculum or Perilous Parasite? Encouraging Genetic Research through Patent Grants: a Call for Regulation and Debate." **San Diego Law Review,** v. 18 (Mar. 1981) pp. 263–299.

Cooper, Iver Peter. **Biotechnology and the Law.** (New York: C. Boardman Co., 1982) 688 p.

Cooper, Iver Peter. "Patent Protection for New Forms of Life. "**Federal Bar Journal,** v. 38, (winter 1979) pp. 34–38.

Darr, Frank P. "Expanding Patent Coverage: Policy Implications of Diamond v. Chakrabarty." **Ohio State Law Journal,** v. 42, no. 4 (1981) pp. 1061–1083.

Grosso, Andrew. "Legislation for the Patenting of Living Organisms: Specificity, Public Safety and Ethical Considerations." **Journal of Legislation,** v. 7 (1980) pp. 113–124.

Hefferon, Thomas J. "Patent Law—Diamond v. Chakrabarty—the U.S. Supreme Court Rules that Living Matter is Patentable." **North Carolina Law Review,** v. 59 (June 1981) pp. 1001–1011.

Kass, Leon R. "Patenting Life." **Journal of the Patent Office Society,** v. 63 (Nov. 1981) pp. 571–600. Also appears in: **Commentary,** v. 72 (Dec. 1981) pp. 45–57.

Krueger, Karen Goodyear. "Building a Better Bacterium: Genetic Engineering and the Patent Law After Diamond v. Chakrabarty. "**Columbia Law Review,** v. 81 (Jan. 1981) pp. 159–178.

Patentability of Microorganisms—Issues and Questions. A public forum sponsored by the American Society for Microbiology, in cooperation with the Committee on Science and Technology, U.S. House of Representatives, and the Congressional Clearinghouse on the Future, 25 July 1980. (Washington: Board of Public and Scientific Affairs, American Society for Microbiology, 1981) 66 p.

Patenting of Life Forms. Edited by David W. Plant, Neils J. Reimers, Norton D. Zinder. (Cold Spring Harbor, N.Y.: Cold Spring Harbor Laboratory, 1982) 337 p. (Banbury report 10)

Pautler, Gene. "Patenting of Life Forms: Where Do We Go From Here?" **Trial,** v. 18 (Apr. 1982) pp. 47–50, 76.

Saliwanchik, Roman. **Legal Protection for Microbiological and Genetic Engineering Inventions.** (Reading, Mass.: Addison-Wesley Pub. Co., 1982) 256 p.

"The Supreme Court and Patenting Life." **Hastings Center Report,** v. 10 (Oct. 1980) 10–15.

COMMERCIALIZATION AND GENERAL APPLICATIONS

"Biotechnology—Seeking the Right Corporate Combinations." **Chemical Week,** v. 129 (Sept. 30, 1981) pp. 36–40.

"Biotechnology Back in the Limelight." **Nature,** v. 283 (Jan. 10, 1980) pp. 119, 122–131.

"Biotechnology Becomes a Gold Rush." **Economist,** v. 279 (June 13, 1981) pp. 81–82, 84–86.

Biotechnology in Canada: Promises and Concerns. (Ottawa: Minister of Supply and Services, 1981) 62 p.

"Biotechnology's Drive for New Products." **Chemical Week,** v. 130 (Feb. 24, 1982) pp. 47–52.

Boly, William. "The Gene Merchants." **California Magazine,** v. 7 (Sept. 1982) pp. 76–79, 170–172, 174–176, 179.

Brownlee, Avin, and Anna W. Crull. **Applied Genetics: A Booming Industry.** (Stamford, Conn.: Business Communications Co., 1981) 310 1. (Business opportunity report, C-032).

Bylinsky, Gene. "DNA Can Build Companies, Too." **Fortune,** v. 101 (June 16, 1980) pp. 144–146, 149, 152, 154.

Cowan, Robert C. "The Revolution in Biotechnology." **Christian Science Monitor** (Oct. 27, 1981) p. 13; (Oct. 28) p. 13; (Oct. 29) pp. 12–13.

Culliton, Barbara J. "Biomedical, Research Enters the Marketplace." **New England Journal of Medicine,** v. 304 (May 14, 1981) pp. 1195–1201.

Culliton, Barbara J. "The Hoechst Department at Mass General." **Science,** v. 216 (June 11, 1982) pp. 1200–1203.

DeYoung, Henry. "Chemical Producers Look Beyond Petroleum." **High Technology,** v. 2 (Sept.-Oct. 1982) pp. 57–63.

"Du Pont: Seeking a Future in Biosciences." **Business Week,** no. 2664 (Nov. 24, 1980) pp. 86–89, 92, 96, 98.

Fox, Jeffrey L. "Biotechnology: A High-stakes Industry in Flux." **Chemical & Engineering News,** v. 60 (Mar. 29, 1982) pp. 10–15.

Fox, Jeffrey L. "Can Academia Adapt to Biotechnology's Lure?" **Chemical & Engineering News,** v. 59 (Oct. 12, 1981) pp. 39–44.

Fox, Jeffrey L. "Genetic Engineering Industry Emerges." **Chemical & Engineering News,** v. 58 (Mar. 17, 1980) 15–23.

Genetic Engineering Applications for Industry. Edited by J. K. Paul. (Park Ridge, N.J.: Noyes Data Corporation, 1981) 580 p. (Chemical technology review, no. 197).

Golden, Frederic. "Shaping Life in the Lab." **Time,** v. 117 (March 9, 1981) pp. 50–54, 57–59.

Gregory, Gene. "Biotechnology—Japan's Growth Industry. **New Scientist,** v. 95 (July 29, 1982) pp. 308–310.

Hartley, Brian, and Robert Walgate. "The Biology Business." **Nature,** v. 283 (Jan. 10, 1980) pp. 122–127.

Hilts, Philip J. "Brave New Science." **Washington Post** (Nov. 1, 1981) pp. A1, A8–A9; (Nov. 2) pp. A1, A10; (Nov. 3) pp. A1, A10 (Nov. 4) pp. A1, A10.

International Resource Development, Inc. Advances in Biotechnology Commercialization. (Norwalk, Conn.: IRD, 1981) 249 1. (Its Report #184)

International Resource Development, Inc. The Genetic Engineering Industry Directory. (Norwalk, Conn.: IRD, 1981) 188 1.

Levin, Morris A., and others. **Applied Genetic Engineering: Future Trends and Problems.** (Park Ridge, N.J.: Noyes Publications, 1983) 191 p.

Li, Veronica Huang, and Sandra Stencel. "Genetic Business." **Congressional Quarterly** (Washington: 1980) 947–964 p. (Editorial research reports, 1980, v. 2, no. 24)

McAuliffe, Sharon, and Kathleen McAuliffe. **Life for Sale.** (New York: Coward, McCann & Geoghegan, 1981) 243 p.

Norman, Colin, and Eliot Marshall. "Boom and Bust in Biotechnology." **Science,** v. 216 (June 4, 1982) pp. 1076–1082.

Nossiter, Daniel D. "Designer Genes." **Barron's,** v. 62 (Feb. 22, 1982) pp. 8–9, 22, 24.

Omenn, Gilbert S. "Taking University Research into the Marketplace." **New England Journal of Medicine,** v. 307 (Sept. 9, 1982) pp. 694–700. R11.B7, v. 307.

Phaff, Herman J. "Industrial Microorganisms." **Scientific American,** v. 245 (Sept. 1981) pp. 77–89.

Sojka, Gary A. "Where Biology Could Take Us." **Business Horizons,** v. 24 (Jan.–Feb. 1981) pp. 60–69.

Steiner, Daniel. "Technology Transfer at Harvard University." **Bioethics Quarterly,** v. 2 (Winter 1980) pp. 203–211.

Wade, Nicolas. "Cloning Gold Rush Turns Basic Biology into Big Business." **Science,** v. 208 (May 16, 1980) pp. 688–692.

GENETICS AND MEDICINE

Baxter, John D. "Recombinant DNA and Medical Progress." **Hospital Practice,** v. 15 (Feb. 1980) pp. 57–67.

"Biotechnology's New Thrust in Antibodies." **Business Week,** no. 2688 (May 18, 1981) pp. 147–148, 150, 154, 156.

Bishop, J. Michael. "Oncogenes." **Scientific American,** v. 246 (Mar. 1982) pp. 80–84, 87–92.

Cassill, Kay. "A Time Clock in Your Genes: Is the Life Cycle Pre-set? **Science Digest,** v. 86 (Oct. 1979) pp. 56–60.

Chedd, Graham. "Genetic Gibberish in the Code of Life. **Science 81,** v. 2 (Nov. 1981) pp. 50–55.

Davies, Owen. "Clones vs. Cancer." **Omni,** v. 4 (Sept. 1982) pp. 89–90, 92.

Deitch, Robert. "Unlocking the Double Helix." **"Harvard Magazine,** v. 83 (July–Aug. 1981) pp. 17–21.

Devoret, Raymond. "Bacterial Tests for Potential Carcinogens." **Scientific American,** v. 241 (Aug. 1979) pp. 40–49.

Ebringer, Alan. "The Link Between Genes and Disease." **New Scientist,** v. 79 (Sept. 21, 1978) pp. 865–867.

Friedman, Milton J., and William Trager. "The Biochemistry of Resistance to Malaria." **Scientific American,** v. 244 (Mar. 1981) pp. 154–155, 158–164.

Fulder, Stephen. "A Pathological Race through Life." **New Scientist,** v. 74 (Apr. 1977) pp. 122–124.

Gershon, Elliot S. "Genetics of the Affective Disorders. **Hospital Practice,** v. 14 (Mar. 1979) pp. 117–122.

Graf, Lloyd H., Jr., "Gene Transformation." **American Scientist,** v. 70 (Sept.– Oct. 1982) pp. 496–505.

Hixson, Joseph. "A New Therapeutic Territory: Gene Mapping." **Therapaeia** (Feb. 1981) pp. 11–14, 16–17, 21–22.

Holiobon, Joan. "Genetics and Cancer Prevention." **Science Forum,** v. 11 (July–Aug. 1978) pp. 17–20.

Lange, Charles F. "Good Genes: Methuselah's Secret." **Chemtech,** v. 9 (Feb. 1979) pp. 114–117.

Milstein, Cesar. "Monoclonal Antibodies." **Scientific American,** v. 243 (Oct. 1980) pp. 66–74.

Rosenfeld, Albert. "Genetics: the Edge of Creation." **Geo, the Earth Diary,** v. 4 (Feb. 1982) pp. 90, 92, 94–96, 98–99, 116–117.

Tiollais, Pierre, Patrick Charnay, and Girish N. Vjas. "Biology of Hepatitis B Virus. **Science,** v. 213 (July 24, 1981) pp. 406–411.

Wetzel, Ronald. "Applications of Recombinant DNA Technology." **American Scientist,** v. 68 (Nov.–Dec. 1980) pp. 664–675.

Williamson, Bob. "Gene Therapy." **Nature,** v. 298 (July 29, 1982) 416–418.

Young, Patrick. "Biomedically, NIH Does More, Better, Than Anyplace Else." **Smithsonian,** v. 10 (Aug. 1979) pp. 42–50.